CON

CONCILIUM 2018/4

The Church of The Future

Edited by

Thierry-Marie Courau, Stefanie Knauss
and Enrico Galavotti

Published in 2018 by SCM Press, 3rd Floor, Invicta House, 108–114 Golden Lane, London EC1Y 0TG.

SCM Press is an imprint of Hymns Ancient & Modern Ltd (a registered charity) 13A Hellesdon Park Road, Norwich NR6 5DR, UK

www.concilium.in
www.concilium.hymnsam.co.uk

ISBN 978 0 334 03155 0

Printed in the UK by
Ashford, Hampshire

Concilium is published in March, June, August, October, December

Contents

Contributors

Editorial

Thinking how the Church needs to change if it is constantly to fulfil its mission better is an activity that has been part of its life since the beginning. At the end of the last Council Karl Rahner regarded this as a task and an opportunity. The current period is marked by a deep cultural crisis across the world, in which we must learn to identify the upheavals taking place, in technology, the economy and society, the appeals to new structures of authority and participatory decision-making, the population movements associated with globalisation, with the distribution of resources, with environmental factors, etc. The Church itself cannot be content to continue as a rigid system, fixed once and for all. It has ceaselessly to find in Him who is its foundation, and in conversations with the worlds it has to engage with, the means to renew itself to fulfil its role of being the universal sacrament of salvation.

There are four parts to this issue: Why and how can we frame the question of the Church of the future? What view of this issue is emerging in the continents of the South? What are the significant fields we must explore to imagine the future? And where can we find an idea that holds everything together? Of course, these reflections make no claim to be exhaustive or to end the building work. They are a first effort and an invitation to go further, in freedom.

The first part seeks to place the framework of reflection on the Church of the future on a plane built partly on theology but also on history and sociology. Christoph Theobald, professor of fundamental and dogmatic theology in the Jesuit Faculties in Paris, introduces this issue by questioning the legitimacy of trying to outline the future shape of the Church. He gives an answer and places himself in the footsteps of Vatican II. By so doing he indicates a path that takes the form of a process of ecclesial conversion in four stages, led by the holy Spirit. This reveals the theological criteria that must accompany this process on a world scale: pastoral concern, reform in the spirit of the Gospel, an ecumenical and missionary character and the charismatic and hierarchical gifts, placed within a process of listening to the faithful.

The Church historian Massimo Faggioli, professor at Villanova University (Philadelphia, USA) carries out a historical and sociological analysis of some tendencies that may be significant for the Church of the future as they build on the openings created by the Second Vatican Council and recently by Pope Francis. He asks about the factors influencing our age, and whether it should be described as a period of transition, touching on cultural plurality, the tragic events that have occurred in the world and the Church, its sociological decline, deinstitutionalisation, the question of the ordained ministry, the place of women, popular culture and the neo-traditionalist reaction.

Part II is an attempt to define a number of turning-points seen from three so-called 'Southern' continents: Asia, Latin America and Africa. The Filipino sociologist, a young researcher at Manila University's Ateneo, Jayeel Cornelio, begins with a consideration of the Church as a worldwide phenomenon. He shows first that the common claim that the new centre of the Church is in the global South has to be qualified. Then he emphasises two challenges: the younger generations and the inequalities that have severe impacts on the present and future life of the planet. The way the Church responds to these challenges will deeply influence its future shape.

Virginia Azcuy, professor of theology at the Catholic University of Buenos Aires (Argentina), currently doing research at the Catholic University of Chile, has chosen to start from the complex and ambiguous reality of the Church today in order to imagine its future. She underlines the tension the institution is experiencing between what it is able to achieve and its aspirations to live its mission to the full. This forces it to face failure and limit. To discern the features of the future Church, Azcuy decides to do practical ecclesiology on three challenges she sees as fundamental: weak credibility, the deformation created by clericalism, male prejudices and spiritual worldliness.

Stan Chu Llo, professor at Chicago's DePaul University, who is doing research on African Catholicism, considers the Church of the future in Africa in the light of Pope Francis' ecclesiology. He reflects on a world Catholicism in which the African churches are playing a significant role in the formation of the identity and mission of the universal Church. He offers the theological outline for a route map for the African church, which, he argues, will have to engage in mission as poor and merciful if it wishes to transform the tragic and unacceptable episodes of the continent's history into eschatological fruits of the Reign of God.

After geographical approaches in which theology combines with sociology, Part III envisages the problems associated with the Church of the future from the point of view of specific disciplines. Mike van Treek Nilsson, a young Chilean biblicist, considers what the bible can contribute to the life of society and a renewal of the Church when approached via an exegesis that takes account of its powerful symbolic imagination. A sapiential, literary and humanistic approach to the bible makes it possible to open up the biblical material and put it in touch with other experiences of God, to initiate conversations with other worlds. The aim is to avoid any form of fundamentalism or instrumentalisation of the bible in order to allow deeper human encounters and recognise God's action in them.

The Italian theologian Serena Noceti, an ecclesiologist and specialist in catechetics, seeks to emphasise how it is necessary and possible to imagine structural transformations of the Church in a period in which we are leaving behind a Euro-centric Church thanks to Pope Francis. This means reshaping roles and functions, powers and their exercise, and the models of communication within the Church. Prophetic initiatives in particular local churches may make it possible to try experiments that could benefit the universal Church's evangelising mission while respecting cultural sensitivities.

The digital world is of particular relevance to the future Church's missionary activity. Daniella Zsupan-Jerome, professor of liturgy and pastoral studies in New Orleans, argues for a proactive presence of the Church in the world of digital communications technologies and the culture they create. This requires attention to three socio-cultural aspects of that world: trust, the possibility of authentic encounters and the overturning of concepts of authority. By stressing the holy Spirit in relation to these three dimensions, she tries to produce a pneumatological foundation for a vision of a Church that bears witness to the Gospel in a voluntary and prophetic way in this digital culture.

Finally, Thierry-Marie Courau, professor of theology at the Institut Catholique in Paris, in search of a keystone that will hold the different elements of this discussion together, suggests that this keystone has to permeate the spirit and the reform of the Church to make it attentive to the calls of the future, and finds it in a listening attitude that unfolds in action. Exactly like the term dia-logue, this concept must become part of the vocabulary of theology and its teachings and become the subject of specific theological research projects, since it is nothing less than the possibility for individuals and communities to attain salvation in their ordinary everyday existence, which is capable of transforming society. This possibility becomes reality, as Pope Francis' popular theology invites us to see, through the eyes and ears of the poorest in society as it leads the Church into a state of *metanoia* through the action of the Spirit.

Professor Courau has just been elected president of *Concilium* in succession to the Indian theologian Felix Wilfred, who filled the role for more than eleven years with great intelligence, clarity of vision and generosity, for which we here offer him our heartfelt thanks.

The Theological Forum in this issue deals with the place of theology at the annual meeting of the American Academy of Religion, and considers the state of theological publishing in continental Europe and the fiftieth anniversary of *Humanae Vitae*.

Translated by Francis McDonagh

Part One: Framework and Method

The Courage to Anticipate the Future of the Church

CHRISTOPH THEOBALD

The article deals with the question of the shape of the Church of the future by tracing a route with crossroads and outlining, in the wake of Vatican II, a process of Church conversion in four stages (with four theological criteria) that will enable tomorrow's Church to appear, the principal architect of which is the holy Spirit. The article puts forward four theological criteria: (1) 'pastorality'; (2) 'Gospel-inspired reform'; (3) ecumenism and mission; (4) 'charismatic and hierarchical gifts', rearranged by the experience of listening to the 'understanding of the faithful' in a synodal process.

Asking questions about the Church of the future might be suspected of being no more than an expression of anxiety from a few Christians on the 'old continent', Europe, troubled by the rapid decline of a brilliant tradition that was once dominant. But the question is also relevant in Africa, Asia and America North and South, though each time in a very specific form and no doubt different from the way it is posed at the heart of Mediterranean culture. Awareness of this diversity makes us recognize the limitations of these brief reflections, but also respect the need to formulate *common* theological criteria that will enable us to outline even now a future vision for the universal Church.

In this spirit I will follow a suggestion made in 1979 by Karl Rahner in an essay proposing 'a fundamental theological interpretation of Vatican II'.[1] Rahner says that previously the Church had experienced only two major transformations in the two millennia of its history, its encounter with Hellenistic and European culture and the still recent birth of a world Christianity. Rahner argues that these two mutations are not just cultural changes, but *events that affect revelation itself*, since the inculturation of Christianity represents a real recreation (*Neuschöpfung*). Vatican II would thus have to be thought of as the first council of a Church on the way to becoming a world Church.

With this in mind, Rahner offers an 'authoritative' theological criterion on the basis of which it is possible to anticipate the Church of the future, but on condition of starting from a future-directed interpretation of the Council and its texts and, above all, accepting surprises from current developments that were not part of Vatican II's 'predictions'. It is not surprising that these two conditions continue to spark far-reaching conflicts within the Church that, if they came to dominate Church life, would risk seriously crippling the creativity of the churches and their ability to think of a future. With these difficulties and conflicts in mind, in this article I shall try to outline four crossroads or alternatives where key decisions about the future are at stake, ranging from the most global and common to the most specific and.[2]

I The tradition of Christianity and the Church as a historical and cultural phenomenon

There are no two ways about it: Vatican II is the first council that took account of the historical nature and the cultural roots of the tradition of Christianity and the Church. And of course, there were difficulties, as shown by the conciliar debates, the course they took right up to the last session (1965), and the problems they left us with.

To mention a few elements, *Dei verbum*, the decree on revelation, was able to absorb the main findings of critical exegesis as it was at the time and put forward a hermeneutic of the scriptures adequate to the sense of history of the day and lay the foundations of a theology of the Christian and Church tradition that gives scope for the current creativity of all those who carry on the tradition. Basing itself on 'the duty of scrutinising the signs of the times and of interpreting them in the light of the Gospel' (GS 4), *Gaudium et spes* began by presenting a careful diagnosis of the current situation (already presupposed in *Lumen gentium*, 1) and went on to discuss the Christian mystery in an anthropological perspective, by the criteria of the modern period, not without criticising them seriously, and even looked in detail at various areas of our life (marriage and family, culture, economy and society, etc.). It was, finally, the decree on the Church's missionary activity, *Ad gentes*, that went furthest in recognising major socio-cultural territories, each with its own history (AG 22).

This new approach can be described by the term 'pastorality', coined by John XXIII. This presupposes a *constitutive* relation between evangelisation *and* those at whom it is directed, and so involves combining a hermeneutic of the Gospel and a hermeneutic of languages and cultures open to receive the Good News of Christ. Two passages show that this principle of 'pastorality' has not only a one-off importance but concerns the whole of Christian tradition in its ability to those who receive it and enter into dialogue with it. The passages are *Gaudium et spes*, 44 and *Ad gentes*, 22, the first of which goes so far as to formulate a law: 'This accommodated preaching (*accommodata praedicatio*) of the revealed word ought to remain the law of all evangelization (*lex omnis evangelizationis*)'.

Here we have *the first of our crossroads*. We increasingly hear, in Europe but also on other continents, voices which base their argument on the perversity of Western modernity or ultra-modernity, criticising its fundamental 'immanentism' and 'individualism', and no longer look in the developments of culture for a 'starting-point' or a 'gap' for 'accommodated preaching'. The tendency then is to abandon Vatican II's double hermeneutic and 'absolutise' the Gospel of God and identify it with the various doctrinal truths contained in the tradition, as found collected in the *Catechism of the Catholic Church* and, in the life of a believer, in a uniform liturgy and, as regards Church procedures, in the *Code of Canon Law*. It is clear that in this paradigm the Church of the future can be no more than a reproduction of the Church of recent centuries.

Pope Francis' speeches and texts, and the last synod of bishops, have brought the question of 'pastorality' back to the foreground of Church debate, and have brought some clarification. This concerns both the relationship between 'doctrine' (in the classical sense of the term) and pastoral ministry, and the historical and cultural plurality of those to whom doctrine is addressed. As for 'pastorality', it must *include* doctrine, but also leaves us with the hermeneutical task of isolating its authoritative element, not in itself, *but in relation with those who whom it is addressed today*; this is what the Apostolic Exhortation *Amoris Laetitia* does for marriage and the family. As for the cultural and historical diversity of those to whom the Gospel is addressed, this is spelt out in the Exhortation *Evangelii Gaudium*. This text contrasts two ways of understanding the relationship to context, the model of 'the sphere, which is no greater than its parts, where every point is equidistant from the centre, and there are no differences between them', and 'the polyhedron, which reflects the convergence of all its parts, each of which preserves its distinctiveness' (EG 236).

What is being outlined here is a change of paradigm: it removes the illusion of a doctrinal, liturgical and juridical equidistance between the Roman centre and the various contexts, allowing for the unpredictable openness of history and to the different time scales of countries and continents, and, as regards the Church of the future, invites us to stand back and watch for the action of the Spirit of Pentecost, one and also many.

II A tripolar vision of God's Gospel, open to the future

Having passed this first crossroads in the direction of 'pastorality' (by no means an obvious choice), we can now see quite plainly the vision of the future Church the Council fathers have given us. It is based on three poles: (1) the ultimate reference point of the Christian faith, the *Gospel of the Kingdom of God*; (2) the *historical situation* of society, which the is the space in which the Gospel may be accepted; and (3) the current *form of the Church*, in other words 'all that she herself is, all that she believes' (DV 8) is entirely marked by its socio-cultural and ecological environment – whether it likes it or not, whether it realizes it or not. In their reciprocal correlation, these three poles define the structure of the tradition (*paradosis*), which is thus composed of a historical series of 'forms', of which the very first is our inspired scriptures, a plural 'form' and one that enjoys chief authority.

The consequence of this structure is the demand for 'continuous reform'. In the form of individual conversion, this has always been implied in the reception of God's Gospel by the virtue of faith. It was not until the second millennium and especially in the 16th century that this principle and the idea of 'reform' of the Church became *intrinsically* connected, precisely in and as result of the Reformation. The Reformation had a critical action and a positive action: it criticized Church 'traditions' (and those of society) for distorting the absolute gratuitousness inherent in the Gospel and becoming self-referential or idolatrous; at the same time, it established a way of believing and living in society and the Church that was based solely on the principle of the Gospel. Whereas the Council of Trent continued to contrast decrees on the faith and others dealing with Church reform, Vatican II connects these two *inseparable* sides of an *Ecclesia semper reformanda* (LG 8 and UR 6) and adds the *relationship with others* within our human societies as an implication of the same Gospel principle. The demand for reform is thus not only a question of the Church's fidelity to the Gospel, but also and in the same movement the expression of its messianic concern for others and for the possibility that they may accept the Gospel. The Church only exists if it is 'decentred' in two ways: towards Christ Jesus and towards all creatures (LG 1): it is in its very make-up 'outgoing', as Pope Francis puts it.

We now come to *another crossroads*. In our increasingly fragmented societies, the theologal vision described above is in danger of being displaced by a short-term pragmatism. Church reform can then be easily reduced to a managerial task, carried out according to 'economic' criteria fashionable in other organisations, mobilizing all the creativity of pastoral workers, even making them excited and giving them a good feeling that they have done something for the benefit of all. In the end, it is a more or less disguised form of ecclesio-centrism and a way of falling in with society's liberal values that come to dominate, and this result is made even worse if it connects with a sort of unconscious 'neo-Darwinism' that, in some circles, is in danger of confusing the number and social and political influence of signed-up Catholics and the fruitfulness of the Gospel. Evidently in this case it is not what the Church or God's Gospel will look like in the future that is the problem; this is treated as given in advance – and often reduced to a set of devotions and a system of values. What obsesses the leaders is the impact of the presence of the Church in society.

On the other side are those who regard the Church first and foremost as a community of disciples of Christ Jesus and therefore as *a space for constant learning*, with the hesitations, failures and welcome surprises that go with this way of being individually and collectively part of an open history. The 'permanent reform' of the Church then has its source in daily listening to the Gospel, reading the scriptures and reading the

17

'signs of the times'. It presupposes a formation, started by the various Catholic Action movements and revived and reformed by Vatican II, with the main aim of learning to combine day by day the two hermeneutics (which we discussed at the first crossroads) and access to an inner life or liturgical prayer, and joining a Church of listening. How, after all, can I hear God's voice if I can't hear my neighbour's? The Church of the future is thus already present in the *shared* desire for a Church life increasingly modelled on the Gospel.

III A diaspora ecumenical Church caring for social ties and the future of creation

The desire just mentioned is the common force that unites Christians of all 'confessions' and makes them feel even more deeply the scandal of their divisions (UR 1). This brings us to a third theological criterion, which adds more detail to the image of the future Church.

The desire for a Church more closely conformed to the Gospel and so more genuinely united emerged in the 19th century and has gone through various stages. The most astonishing evolution has taken place in the Catholic Church, which, in the space of only 36 years, has gone from the 'unionism' reaffirmed in 1928 by the encyclical *Mortalium animos*, which severely condemned the early conferences of the ecumenical movement, to the Decree *Unitatis redintegratio* of 1964, which, on the contrary, saw this movement as an appeal of the Spirit. Our first criterion reveals that the historical causes of these surprising developments are very significant:3 the crisis of faith produced by the *Gott mit uns*, 'God with us', attitude of the first world war was followed by new social challenges like the various technological, socio-political and cultural revolutions with their gradual waves of de-Christianisation, laicization and secularization, 'welcomed' of course in different ways by the denominations, but gradually creating a new Christian solidarity: the weakening of each individual and each 'denomination' was first endured before being understood as part of the Gospel condition and being heard as a call to meet other Christians and Christians in different situations.

A differently shaped Church starts to appear at Vatican II. It is based on the diaspora status of Christian communities that have left behind the age of Christendom (LG 26) but moved by the appeal to work for the unity of all the disciples of Christ Jesus (UR 5) and to join in the Church's missionary activity (LG 17; AG 6.6): 'the preaching of the Gospel to the whole of creation'. If the diaspora status of Christians is confirmed today over most of the world, ecumenism and missionary activity took on new and unexpected dimensions at Vatican II, and it is these that we have a duty to project into the future.

We have now reached a *third crossroads*. It is not surprising that the diaspora situation of many Christians provokes sectarian retreats. Some people try to escape from the 'ghetto' by joint social action (for example, on behalf of refugees and asylum-seekers), leaving 'doctrinal' differences on one side. Others, in contrast, wait for Church unity to be achieved by future doctrinal agreements between experts and senior Church leaders, at the risk of seeing their hopes fade into the distance and giving up hope of the ecumenical cause.

Here the anticipation of the shape of tomorrow's Church means treating the call to ecumenism and the call to mission as *one*. Mission certainly involves in the first place a significant presence of Christians and their communities in society as it is today, which is very different from what it was in 1965. The Catholic Church has also corrected some anthropocentric and very general ideas found in *Gaudium et spes*, and now interprets 'living together' (*Evangelii Gaudium*), affected by all sorts of violence, and 'care for the common home' (*Laudato si'*) as 'signs of the times' with a particular Gospel insistence on listening to what is weak, to the poor (in all senses of the term) *and* to creation. In contrast, some areas, such as equality between women and men, remain curiously 'under-exposed'.

However this may be, the holy Spirit, who is assumed to be present in what is identified as a 'sign of the times', calls Christian communities to question themselves in the Church learning space (the one that started at the second crossroads) about their interpretation of the Gospel of the Kingdom of God and of creation that has to be heard today, *and* about the shape of the Church, which has to be adapted to the here and now, *and to do this together*. This shows clearly the intrinsic link between the call to mission and the call to unity, heard as long ago as the 1910 Edinburgh assembly. For if all Christians are part of a common history, this means that a common interpretation of the Gospel received from the tradition will be made possible by the need to proclaim it (1 Cor 9.16) loudly, not just

19

in actions – by a 'presence' in society – but also in words. As regards the shape of the Church of the future, the questions that come from society are both very specific, for example, on the place of women in the government of the communities – and fundamental: if the route to visible unity does not include a 'return' (to Rome or Constantinople) or a simple ecumenical federation, what *conversion of our images of visible unity* can be set in train by this 'neither…nor' of 'a negative ecclesiology' that will do justice to our desire to reach a communion of pulpit and eucharistic table?[4]

IV For a Church founded on the charisms of all, the 'sense of the faithful', apostolicity and synodality

We now face the specific, detailed question of the visible shape of tomorrow's Church. There can be no doubt that we must put more work, with Orthodoxy and some Protestant movements, into the pneumatological renewal of the Church, an outline of which is already present in the Constitution *Lumen gentium*, 4: 'The Spirit guides the Church into all truth and unifies it in communion and in works of ministry. He both equips and directs it with hierarchical and charismatic gifts and adorns it with his fruits (cf. Eph 4, 11-12; 1 Cor 12, 4; Gal 5, 22).'

Signs of a structure in tension are visible here and in the rest of the Constitution. It connects the Pauline vision of the charisms and the faithful's 'sense of the faith' (*supernaturalis sensus fidei*, LG 12), the apostolic and collegial charism (LG 19, 20, 24) and, more discreetly, the institution of the synod (CD 5, 36; OE 9, etc).[5] At the synod on the family, however, Pope Francis 'resited' these four poles on the basis of 'synodality, a constitutive element of the Church,' which, he said, 'offers us the most appropriate interpretive framework for understanding the hierarchical ministry itself". 'A synodal Church,' said the Pope, is a Church that listens' (Address to commemorate the 50th Anniversary of the Institution of the Synod of Bishops, 17 October 2015).

There is one last crossroads on our road towards the Church of the future. It is understandable that this papal 'rearrangement' should provoke resistance, because the hierarchical structure that gradually became the norm in post-Tridentine and Vatican Christendom has great potentialities for administrative efficiency and still reassures many believers. But it may fail to see the spiritual 'phreatic tables' hidden in our contemporary societies that emerge in the 'charisms' with which many believers are endowed, or which they themselves *are* for others (*charismaticos*, LG 7.3). This is therefore a new spiritual demand – a sort of nudge from the Spirit – appearing at this point in the polyhedral history of the Church: the disappearance of the 'cleric' in favour of a 'hierarchical' ministry, which, at all levels in the Church, ('as though in an upside-down pyramid') will be exercised like the work of a water diviner (cf *Presbyterium ordinis*, 6.2) to release each person's unique vocation and his or her ability to serve others, listening to each other and discussing together (ecumenically) the directions to take… 'until the Lord comes' (1 Cor 11.26).

*

It will be clear that I have not produced a 'plan' for the Church of the future, but instead suggested a route with crossroads and outlined, in the wake of Vatican II, a process of Church conversion in four stages (with four theological criteria) that will enable tomorrow's Church to appear. The principal architect is the holy Spirit. In the current difficulties and confusions, which I have tried to take seriously, such a route map may be of more use, though it can never replace the inner compass within each of us and within the body of believers. So we are left with the question Luke's Jesus dared to put to the people of his day: 'When the Son of Man comes, will he find faith on earth?' (Lk 18.8). It remains as relevant as ever.

Translated by Francis McDonagh

Christoph Theobald

Notes

1. Karl Rahner 'A fundamental theological interpretation of Vatican II', in Lucien Richard et. al. (ed) *Vatican II: The Unfinished Agenda: A Look to the Future* (New York, 1987).
2. For more details, cf C. Theobald, *Urgences pastorales du moment présent. Pour une pédagogie de la réforme*, Paris, 2017.
3. Cf Etienne Fouilloux, *Les catholiques et l'unité chrétienne du XIXe au XXe siècle. Itinéraires européens d'expression française*, Paris, 1982.
4. Cf C. Theobald, 'Le courage d'anticiper un avenir commun. L'unité visible de l'Eglise, à quelles conditions ?', *Irénikon* 90 (2017/1), 5-31.
5. See the two issues of *Recherches de Science Religieuse* on 'apostolicity' (103 [2015/2]) and on the 'sense of the faith, sense of the faithful' (104 [2016/2]).

The Church of the Future: Historical and Sociological Perspectives

MASSIMO FAGGIOLI

This article seeks to analyse some guiding tendencies for the church of the future starting out from the trajectories opened by the Second Vatican Council and taken up again recently by Pope Francis. Even though there are different local situations, some questions are common to the whole of the global church: a conception of leadership not isolated from the ordained ministry; a vision of ministry of the church as service; the role of women in the ecclesial community. Recent years have highlighted two contrasting thrusts: a globalization of the church and at the same time within the church, too, a crisis of globalization (and not only religious) in the form of a return of phenomena of neo-traditionalist reactions, in more than just liturgical matters, which it would be inappropriate to underestimate and consider as fleeting manifestations destined to disappear quickly.

I Introduction

In a period in which different and sometimes conflicting narratives continue to emerge about Catholicism's past, dependent on the opinions and places from which these narratives emerge, it is essential to raise the question of the church of the future. But any reflection about the church of the future, in other words the possible developments of the object church in the time to come, must be rooted in an historical analysis. For a community and an institution such as the church, the element of tradition is still decisive, and despite tradition and history not identifying with each other, tradition cannot be understood – either retrospectively in the past or prospectively in the future – without history. There are some questions which stand out as preliminaries.

II Historical perspective: from Vatican II to the difficult start of the 21st century

The first question is about the framework of the contemporary church in a broad historical time span. The periodization of the contemporary church cannot set aside the event of the Second Vatican Council (1962-1965): the church of today is living a post-conciliar conciliar religious culture and theology which have different characteristics from the pre-conciliar ones.[1] But the question of periodization must tackle the question of the relationship between that periodizing event and the previous Tridentine paradigm: in other words, as Paolo Prodi has underlined, the question is whether the Second Vatican Council opened a new era, in which the church finds itself today, or whether the Second Vatican Council simply closed the preceding Tridentine period, inaugurating not a new era but only a transition towards a new period not yet realised.[2]

A second question concerns the plurality of paradigms. If, in the Tridentine paradigm, we can speak of a church which at least in theory believed in a strong unity and uniformity of social and cultural models, for the post-conciliar period it is necessary to begin to speak about not just *de facto* but also *de iure* theological, cultural and social pluriformity. The post-conciliar church consists of different models or of a diversity which increases: between different churches in different nations, between different regions within the same country, between different ecclesial communities within the same local church.[3]

A third essential historical question which gives rise to reflection on the church of the future concerns the periodization of the post-conciliar era, in other words, whether there are and what different periods marked by different characteristics would be, in the history of the church starting from the start of the conciliar event, with its convocation by John XXIII almost sixty years ago. From this point of view, we can ask whether the change of century did not coincide with new period within the history of the conciliar reception. In different ways and on different levels, the coming to light of the sex abuse crisis in the United States between 2001 and 2002 and the wars caused by the terrorist attacks of 11 September 2001 contributed to the emergence of a new type of awareness in the relationship between religions and global politics and therefore also a different awareness in and of the church. It is not just a new century with features different from

24

those expected and expressed by official Catholicism (John Paul II's Apostolic Letter *Tertio Millennio Adveniente*, 1994, and the Great Jubilee of the year 2000), but also a different post-conciliarism, or a 'second post-conciliarism' which opens with the transition from the generation of the conciliar leaders to the generation of Catholics born and brought up in the post-conciliar period. Among the characteristics of this new awareness there is a different relationship with the contemporary world – from the new relationship between the church and secularity of Vatican II to the secularised and post-secular world of the 21st century.[4]

III Between sociological decline, de-institutionalization and neo-traditional revival

The situation of the current church is marked by some characteristics which have been consolidated in the post-conciliar era, which we can only outline here in general terms.

A sociological decline of the church in the north-western hemisphere is obvious: a fall in the percentage of the baptized and Mass-goers in the churches in Europe and in North America – a fall which in North America especially is masked by the influx of Catholic immigrants especially from central and southern America, and in Europe, too, to a lesser extent, by the influx of Christian immigrants or refugees from Eastern Europe, the Middle East, and Africa. This decline implies less influence of the church in popular culture and in legislation, a political scattering of the Catholic electorate into different parties and movements, and a weakening of Catholic institutions (schools, hospitals, associations, parties and unions) in the countries where the welfare system does not need to rely on Catholic institutions subsidised by the state. Even more visible is the number of ordained ministers of worship and members of male and female religious Orders, compared to the first half of the twentieth century.

This has meant a re-distribution of leadership tasks in the church: in favour of the male permanent diaconate reinstated by Vatican II (with a great number of deacons especially in some countries, like the United States), in favour of male and female laity (some but not all with professional formation), and in favour of new lay movements. But this redistribution has taken place in the absence of a real discussion about the future of ministry (ordained and non-ordained, female and male) in the church, in defence of an apparently unchanged model of priestly and sacred ministry, male and celibate. A plurality of ministries and of ministerial figures has been inaugurated largely *extra legem*, forced by emergency circumstances and made possible (when possible) by the financial resources of local churches able to take on lay personnel (male and female) to positions of pastoral care which in other times were entrusted exclusively to clergy.

Alongside this situation of sociological decline and re-definition of the profiles of ministry consideration must be given at the global level to the institutional and 'political' persistence in the broad sense of the church and the churches.[5] The post-conciliar and contemporary face of the church is always that of a church active on the front of human rights (of human beings as such, not as belonging to a particular church or religious community) and of a *welfare state* supplementing some of the gaps created by neo-liberal politics, both at the level of *advocacy* by the papacy and by the Holy See, and at the level of the epsicopates, the clergy, and local associations.

This profile of movements in the current church must reconcile itself with a great diversification of models of church which show signs of the different models of the relationship between state and church (in the *continuum* which goes from the classic concordat model of the 'state church' to that of the clandestine and persecuted church, passing through the various separationist models). This diversity of models contributes to shaping the different styles of church: from a 'culture war' style of church combative through legal means on the front of sensitive bioethical issues (like that of the United States) to that of dialogue with republican secularism (as in France) or constitutional patriotism (as in Germany), to that coming to grips with mediation for the opening of a new phase in relationships between the Holy See and the government, with important repercussions on the internal balances to the local church (as in the People's Republic of China).

These institutional models are all under pressure from a Christianity and a religion which is increasingly less dependent on the religious institution. The contemporary 'age of anger' is also a religious phenomenon, and a subsequent phase of the *'revanche de Dieu'* about which Gilles Kepel spoke in the early 1990s.[6] In the last fifteen years especially, starting out from English-speaking Catholicism, there has been a neo-traditionalist revival, sign of an anti-conciliar reflux in the West: in part a re-balancing of the modernizing and functionalist incentives of the post-conciliar period and of the generation of the baby boomers, in part a reaction to the expansive push of secularization and of Islam in Europe and in the West.

IV Prospectvie trends: doctrine – life – worship

One of the ways of analysing the possible prospective trends is to adopt the doctrine-life-worship trio, the three ways of tradition, from paragraph 8 of Vatican II's Constitution on Revelation, *Dei Verbum*. The central question has come back to being that of different ways of understanding tradition, from which derives the renewed centrality of *Dei Verbum* in the debate on conciliar reception.[7]

From the doctrinal point of view, the transition from the pontificates of John Paul II and Benedict XVI to that of Francis has signified an official approval, symbolically and institutionally, of the transition (already begun at a cultural and theological level) from a Roman, European, and Western model to a multicentric model no longer dominated by an historical-geographic criterion descending from medieval Christianity. This transition has already had an impact on exegesis, Christology, ecclesiology, moral theology and on questions of gender and the future structure of ministerial life in the global church. But the doctrinal future of Catholicism depends on the solution which will be given by magisterium and theology to the question of the Second Vatican Council as an event which marked a passage; in other words, it depends on the path which global Catholicism will take after Francis' pontificate, which has interpreted in an obvious manner an open hermeneutic of the Council.

Much more obvious and less dependent on doctrinal policy, at the current time, are the on-going tendencies from the point of view of the life of the church and of worship. From the point of view of the church's life, the prospective trends suggest a new season in relations between vocation to the ministry and states of life, in the direction of an overcoming of the binary model between ordained priestly ministry and the lay state of life. The church has already recovered in different forms and through initial recognitions (such as the permanent diaconate) a plurality of vocations and ministries more faithful to the church of the origins and less indebted to the ecclesiology of the second millennium. The ministeriality of the male and female religious Orders of the second millennium is being re-distributed within other forms of community and associated life (associations and movements) which envisage greater integration, not a separation between ecclesial vocation and the lay life.

The question of church *governance* requires a broader discussion: centre and margins, people of God and ministries.[8] There is no doubt that one of the long-term ecclesiological trajectories for the Catholic church is the synodal model: in the church there are some issues which merit being the object of a broad process of reflection and discernment which involve clergy and laity, especially women. During the first years of his pontificate, Pope Francis de-centralized authority as judges for briefer processes in marriage annulment cases to local bishops, and the translation of liturgical texts, apart from the *confirmatio* (no longer a *recognitio*) on the part of the Apostolic See, to national bishops' conferences. But it is challenge which goes beyond the episcopal element. The non-episcopal element of the Catholic church (priests, monks and brothers/sisters in religious Orders, male and female lay people) have received ever fewer opportunities to express their views on some urgent issues. The greater urgency to consult the church has until now corresponded to an increasing unwillingness to do so on the part of the institutional church.

It is not a problem dependent solely on post-conciliar doctrinal politics. The debates and final documents approved at the Second Vatican Council frame the life of the church in strongly institutional terms: a church whose leadership was clerical, whose articulation was more territorial than personal, whose public position was both partner and counterpart to the nation state which between the 19th and 20th centuries replaced the empires. And therefore an institution which at Vatican II was changing, but whose role was not at all different from the role that the institution had for the members of the Church in the previous centuries. It seems necessary to re-discover the complex inter-penetration of institutional and communion aspects of the Catholic church. A purely communion-based and congregational Catholic church is something which is not appropriate to the concrete and historical experience of the members of the Roman Catholic Church: one thinks of the need to monitor experiences of abuse, sexual or otherwise, within the church. This is not an invitation to maintain the status quo, in other words to over-institutionalise the life of the

Church. The *communio ecclesiarum* is now a more important dimension than before, not just because of the magnitude of the globalization of the Catholic Church, but also because of the quality of this globalization. It is the Catholic church turning towards the south of the world, but also towards a world which is more urbanized than before, where the existential quality of a life of faith is lived above all in urban contexts. The cosmopolitan experience of Pope Francis, the first pope born in a twentieth-century megalopolis, expresses Catholicism's transition to a new understanding of the interpenetration of religious and secular, of global and local, in a multiplicity of diversity.

If the need for the strengthening of the middle level of ecclesial authority between the local (diocesan) and the universal (Rome) is clear, that is the continental and the national, there is a crucial aspect for the future relations between the centre and the margins which Vatican II did not tackle, and on which the post-Vatican II theological debate has been cautious if not circumspect. This is the need to imagine the future of the conciliar dimension of the Catholic church, that is a church where the bishops with right of participation and vote in a general council number more than five thousand. A further problem is that almost half of all Catholic bishops today are titular or emeritus bishops. It is not just a question of the logistical problems of a council with thousands of participants (now almost double compared to the bishops at Vatican II) and of technological solutions to this problem, but also a question of doing it in such a way that the council remains a spiritual and sacramental act which cannot be reduced to a video conference, to a 'WikiCouncil' or a '*concilium cyberspatiale primum*'. It is essentially a question of theology of ecclesiological representation, and not one of jurisprudence.[9]

This question of representation and ecclesial representation has to be understood in the framework of the upheaval of the social, political but also theological concept of 'people'. The nineteenth and twentieth centuries were the era of the mobilisation of the masses in the new national states as well as in the Church. That era has been replaced by a much more fragmented social and ecclesial body. It was easy to identify the Catholic elite with the clergy, the intellectual Catholics and the Catholic political leaders. It was usual to see members of the Catholic lay élite involved in politics, in the world of business, in culture and in the academic world in the lay leadership of the Catholic church. Now the clergy's role as guide is in profound difficulty, and there are Catholic lay leaders whose voices count more than many bishops and cardinals together, but who are no longer part of the old Catholic lay élite. This is one of the effects of the twentieth-century crisis of the theology of the laity.[10] On the other hand, the 'people' are still important for the church but much more as a theological idea (the people of God) than as a homogeneous and socially tangible reality. Ideologically, socially, and ethnically fragmented, globalised Catholicism must take into account the need to re-define who are its people and its peoples.

The theology of priesthood and methods of priestly formation and selection have not changed in these last fifty years. In general it is the true meaning of leadership of the church and of the people of the church which has changed in a significant way. Suffice here to note the profound and probably irretrievable crisis of identification between clergy and leadership of the church. The second millennium saw this leadership being created, starting with the 'Gregorian revolution' of the eleventh century. The third millennium will probably free itself from this identification: in part recognizing the theology lived by our communities, and discussing theologically and ecclesiologically the need for a re-definition of leadership and of ministry in the Church.[11]

Finally, on the question of worship the question must be asked if we are not in the presence of a new phase of the liturgical movement, in the light of the divisive character of the liturgical question which arises from the reduction of the theology of tradition to traditionalism. Benedict XVI's Motu Proprio *Summorum Pontificum* (2007), a document which liberalized the use of the Roman liturgy prior to the reforms begun by the Second Vatican Council (1962-65), significantly changed the situation and therefore also the question about liturgical traditionalism in the Catholic church. *Summorum Pontificum* strengthened the pre-existing and sociologically limited world of liturgical traditionalism and cast it onto the wider world of the Catholic church, especially in the English-language context. It gave theological legitimacy to traditionalist points of view about the liturgical reforms of Vatican II. It increased the visibility of the traditionalist liturgy in virtual spaces and not just that of the Catholic church. This has had a significant impact on considerable parts of contemporary and future Roman Catholicism, above all on young committed Catholics and on *born again* Catholics or recent converts from other Christian traditions (especially from the churches of the Protestant Reformation), as well as on seminary students and young priests.

There is a link between the resurgent liturgical traditionalism and the crisis of globalization and universalism within Catholicism. Vatican II and the theology of the liturgy of the Council are part of this reaction against an inculturation which is not the culture of medieval Latin Catholicism and the Counter-Reformation. The re-birth of traditionalism is typical of all religions in the 'post-secular' era, and Catholicism is no exception: Catholic neo-traditionalism goes way beyond the historical-cultural confines in which the schism of Marcel Lefebvre was born immediately after Vatican II, and it is possible that through *Summorum Pontificum* a new phase in the history of the liturgical movement has been opened. The real question is that of the link between liturgical traditionalism and the negative effects on the acceptance of other documents of Vatican II, such as that on ecumenism, on inter-religious dialogue, on the Church's missionary activity, but also on the theology of revelation and on ecclesiology.

V The post-conciliar 'Weltkirche' and the neo-traditionalist reaction

Despite the legitimate reprimands of conciliar theology about the silencing or reduction of the conciliar stimuli on the part of the ecclesiastical institution, it is difficult to deny that the current Catholic church is largely the church of Vatican II: the new Catholic *establishment* is the fruit of Vatican II. This establishment finds itself faced with a neo-traditionalist reaction which is not a revolution, but nor is it a fleeting revolt.

The church of the future will have to take into account the neo-traditionalist reaction which became clear during the pontificate of Benedict XVI and of Francis. It is a reaction which has its capital in English-speaking Catholicism, animated by different elements in a complex relation between them. There is the theological element, that of the post-liberal theological project, which in America finds its voice in one of the ecumenical observers at Vatican II, George Lindbeck (1923-2018), which is spreading from the Lutheran church to Catholicism, where it finds a more stable home. A second element is that of the evangelicalization of

Catholicism in response to the complexity of conciliar and post-conciliar theology and its 'concessions' to secular modernity. A third element is that of a Catholicism of the anti-institutional conservative revolt which sees in the Catholic establishment – institutional and cultural – and in its weaknesses (with regard to the crisis of sexual abuse, of secularisation, of Islam) an establishment created by the Council and by the post-Council period, and which should therefore be knocked down and re-built once the new clerical ranks, formed by the neo-traditionalist culture of the seminaries, have replaced the generation of twentieth-century priests and bishops. A fourth element is the Catholic criticism of globalization as globalism, which takes the shape of an anti-internationalism which often becomes ethno-nationalism and nativism. It is the crisis of nineteenth-century Catholic internationalism, legacy of nineteenth-century ultramontanism and papalism. This Catholic anti-internationalism assumes the cultural and theological superiority of the culture of the Europe of medieval Christianity and of the Christian West, against economic and financial globalization but also against the globalization of Catholicism.

This neo-traditionalist reaction, in various forms, is a minor phenomenon but it will be difficult to re-absorb without any shock: *mainstream* conciliar Catholicism is no longer the form of Roman Catholicism, or it is a *mainstream* which still exists but only as one of the possible forms of contemporary global Catholicism. In this situation the process of conciliar reception encounters a resistance which has become stronger in the course of the last fifteen years and has become visible through opposition to the pontificate of Francis.

It is not clear if this passage of the conciliar reception will mean a church permanently divided, with what kind of internal division, or a church cast backwards towards a revision of conciliar theology. This latter scenario is intellectually difficult to imagine, given the foundational character of conciliar theology for the whole of the magisterium and post-conciliar theology.

VI Conclusion

The pontificate of Francis has re-opened the question of the future of the church from many points of view: from that of the globalization and diversification of Catholicism, to that of the relationship with tradition.

The church is 'outward looking' not just from the centre to the margins, but also outward looking from the historical-cultural paradigms which had been assumed as definitive. It is a moving scenario which, to be interpreted, calls for a long-term historical vision along with an approach capable of discerning the new global dimension which represents the real unknown with respect to the future of the church.

Translated by Liam & Patricia Kelly

Massimo Faggioli

Notes

1. Cf. *Storia del concilio Vaticano II*, ed. G. Alberigo, Italian edition ed. A. Melloni, 5 volumes, Bologna: Il Mulino, 1995-2001 (translated into English [*History of Vatican II*, 5 volumes, Orbis Books, New York, 1995-2006], French, German, Castillian, Portuguese, Russian); John W. O'Malley, *What Happened at Vatican II*, Cambridge MA: Harvard UP, 2008 (translated into Italian, French, Spanish, Portuguese, Polish, Hungarian).
2. Cf. P. Prodi, *Il paradigma tridentino. Un'epoca della storia della Chiesa*, Brescia: Morcelliana, 2010; P. Prodi, 'Senza Stato né Chiesa. L'Europa a cinquecento anni dalla Riforma', *Il Mulino*, 1/ 2017, pp. 7-23 (English translation 'Europe in the Age of the Reformations. The Modern State and Confessionalization', in *The Catholic Historical Review*, vol. 103, n. 1, Winter 2017, pp. 1-19).
3. Cf. *Zeiten der pastoralen Wende? Studien zur Rezeption des Zweiten Vatikanums – Deutschland und die USA im Vergleich*, eds A. Henkelmann and G. Sonntag, Münster: Aschendorff 2015.
4. Cf. C. Taylor, *A Secular Age*, Cambridge MA: Harvard UP, 2007.
5. Cf. D. Hollenbach, *The Global Face of Public Faith: Politics, Human Rights, and Christian Ethics*, Washington, D.C.: Georgetown UP, 2003.
6. Cf. G. Kepel, *La Revanche de Dieu. Chrétiens, juifs et musulmans à la reconquête du monde, Paris: Seuil, 1991; P. Mishra,* Age of Anger: A History of the Present, New York: Farrar, Straus and Giroux, 2017.
7. Cf. C. Theobald, *La Réception du Concile Vatican II. Vol. I: Accéder à la source*, Paris: Cerf, 2009; C. Theobald, *'Dans les traces...' de la constitution 'Dei Verbum' du concile Vatican II: Bible, théologie et pratiques de lecture*, Paris: Cerf, 2009.
8. A broad range of proposals (30 chapters from 30 different authors from all over the world) in *La riforma e le riforme nella chiesa,* eds. A. Spadaro e C.M. Galli, Brescia: Queriniana, 2016 (Spanish translation Bilbao: Sal Terrae, 2017; English translation New York: Paulist Press, 2017).
9. Cf. S. Dianich, 'Primato e collegialità episcopale: problemi e prospettive', in *La riforma e le riforme nella Chiesa*, 271-292.
10. Cf. M. Vergottini, *Il cristiano testimone. Congedo dalla teologia del laicato.* Preface by Franco Giulio Brambilla, Bologna: EDB, 2017.
11. Cf. *A Church with Open Doors: Catholic Ecclesiology for the Third Millennium*, eds. R.R. Gaillardetz and E.P. Hahnenberg, Collegeville MN: Liturgical Press, 2015.

Part Two: Global Perspectives

The Global Challenges of the Church of the Future

JAYEEL CORNELIO

This article presents the global challenges that matter to the Church of the future. The first part traces the different facets of the Church as a global phenomenon. It complicates the prevailing view that Christianity is moving to the global south. The second part focuses on two challenges: generational shifts and global inequality. While not exhaustive, the discussion will provide some nuances regarding the issues at stake at a global level. The character of the Church of the future rests on how it responds to these present-day issues that will linger in the years ahead.

I Introduction

There are two master narratives concerning the future of Christianity. One is optimistic, the other pessimistic. The optimistic outlook claims that the Church will emerge triumphant. Against all odds, the Church will fulfil its divine mandate to evangelize and convert. The pessimistic view, on the other hand, anticipates its inevitable decline. It contends that Christianity, like any religion, will lose its influence in the future.

Prophetic visions of the Church are repeatedly rehearsed depending on one's religious predispositions. But convictions are not enough in thinking about its future. One reason is that the Church is not a monolithic institution. A sociological view sees it not as a mystical body of Christ, but organizational configurations that take different forms as local congregations, denominations, parishes, and bureaucracies. Christianity, in addition, has many traditions. The most dominant is Catholicism, which constitutes 50% of the world's Christian population of more than 2 billion.[1] Protestantism and Orthodox Christianity constitute 37% and 12%, respectively. 1% come from other Christian groups. Individuals in these communities have theological persuasions and practices that compete with one another. The movement of people and ideas brings these tensions all the more to the surface, which is why it is more useful to talk about global Christianities in the plural.[2]

At the same time the Church is embedded in a wider environment. This means that inasmuch as it proclaims timeless truths, it has to contend with broader changes at the level of society. This is why social contexts need to be factored in when trying to understand the place of the Church in the future. These contexts are social concerns of continuing importance for society and religion. They are arenas of uncertainty. Scholars in foresight studies maintain that uncertainty, which 'problematizes decision making in the present', can inform what is said about the future and how it is to be achieved.[3] While spelling out these contexts in full is impossible, a few are identifiable that will remain compelling in the years to come.

The social contexts I intend to discuss here are salient qualities of global society: inequality and generational shifts. These are two of the global challenges of the Church. They present themselves as opportunities for the Church to lend its institutional and cultural resources.[4] Indeed, it needs to exert its influence because the way global society is mostly organized by secular institutions sidesteps the potential contributions of religion.[5] At the same time, this approach is in keeping with the view that the Church is a global phenomenon. It is a complex institution, alongside businesses, non-government organizations, and other actors in civil society that make globalization possible.

This article proceeds as follows. The first part will deal with the global condition of Christianity. It spells out the different facets of the Church as a global phenomenon. It complicates the prevailing view that Christianity is moving to the global south. The second part will focus on two inescapable challenges: generational shifts and global inequality. While not exhaustive, their respective discussions will provide some nuances regarding the issues at stake at a global level. Taken together, these challenges reveal the limits of globalization as a hopeful process. And yet they point back to the potential contributions of the Church. Thus the shape of the Church of the future is yet to be seen. While Christian thought offers a triumphalist eschatology, the Church of the future, in a sociological sense, is instead actively achieved. Put differently, the Church of the future is not a given; it has to be imagined and constructed if it were to be desirable.

II Church as a global phenomenon

A common theme in writings about the future of Christianity is that it is moving to the global south, which roughly constitutes Latin America, Asia, and Africa. The projection is that by 2050, 72% of Christians will come from these regions.[6] Although this view has become commonplace, it needs to be interrogated. The most recent statistical data show that by 2060, Christianity will maintain its global proportion of 31.8%. It was 31.2% in 2015. What supports the claim is the noticeable decline in Europe from 24% to 14% and in North America from 12% to 9%.

But the growth is uneven in the global south. The biggest growth for Christianity will take place among the people of sub-Saharan Africa from 26% to 42% in the same period. By contrast, the same growth is not expected in Latin America where in fact it goes down from 25% to 22% and in the Asia-Pacific where it remains unchanged at only 13%. At the same time the claim overlooks the trends in other religions. Islam's global proportion, for example, will pick up its pace from 24.1% to 31.1%, thus matching Christianity by 2060.[7]

In this regard the claim that the Church is moving to the global south puts aside crucial nuances. It is also analytically problematic. The north-south divide is, for one, geographically inaccurate. A big proportion of countries in Asia is in the northern hemisphere. Moreover the divide reeks of ethnocentrism. That Christianity grows in the global south is associated with economic backwardness. It is not surprising, for example, that Pentecostalism, which is quite expansive in these regions, is wrongly associated with only the poor. To illustrate, Pentecostalism takes different forms around the world. El Shaddai, a charismatic group in the Philippines, is a gathering of urban poor Catholics. And yet there are many other charismatic fellowships that attract middle-class young professionals in the country and elsewhere.

Thus a re-orientation is needed in understanding the state of the Church. The global connections and tensions need to be investigated carefully; Christianity is not strictly confined to national configurations. One way of thinking about this point is in terms of religious networks.

Missionary networks are not only regional in orientation. The movement of missionaries remains global. While many missionaries still come from North America, as in the case of Protestant groups, missionary networks have become diverse. The phenomenon of postcolonial missionary work is a good example. In many cases these are pastors who come from postcolonial societies to minister to their own people who have migrated to, say, Europe. This of course does not discount the big role of African and Asian clergy serving in Western congregations.

The global connections are also in terms of congregational and even parachurch alliances. The most obvious example is represented by international Bible societies that are very ecumenical in character. Catholic and Protestant groups in different countries work together to publish and distribute Bibles around the world. Megachurches are another example. They are part of global alliances that make possible the circulation of their preachers and worship leaders. As a result, these religious groups adopt the same theological persuasions and even the same repertoire of songs. Similarly, religious networks sustain global religious events. While clearly initiated by the Catholic Church, the World Youth Day is a prime example of a global event that attracts youth from different religious backgrounds. The success of the event relies on wide networks of youth workers, an obvious manifestation of the global scale of contemporary Christianity.

But the significance of global religious networks for the life of the Church is not only about scale. These networks make it possible for religious movements to emerge. Charismatic Christianity is a very good example of a religious movement that influences parishes and congregations of different traditions around the world. It relies on complex networks of evangelists, seminaries, publications, and websites. The same can be said of social movements related to such issues as climate change, human rights, and religious freedom. Faith-based activists rely on global networks to address what they believe are issues about which the Church cannot be silent.[8] Global networks are thus not only about expanding institutional membership. They make more pronounced the ability of local communities to respond collectively to global concerns. The character of the Church of the future rests on how its actors are able to do so.

III Global challenges

The previous section discussed how far the Church is a global phenomenon. This section discusses two of its global challenges: generational shifts and global inequality. They are constellations of present-day concerns already affecting the Church. But because they are long-term concerns they also provide various possibilities for the Church. That these challenges are global also means that the Church of the future will continue to assert its global presence through its reaction to these challenges.

The point is that the influence of the Church is not a given; it is achieved. After all, religious communities must 'reflect on globalisation by filtering its perceived impact on their activities and place in the world'.[9] This section is not an exhaustive discussion of all the challenges in a global context but are illustrative of global concerns that affect not just Christianity but also other religions and social spheres. Other scholars have focused instead on specifically religious issue such as, say, interreligious tensions.[10]

(a) Generational shifts

The first global challenge has to do with generational shifts; age patterns have social consequences. The median age of Christians around the world is 30, which is a little above the overall median age of 28.[11] One can say that Christians are generally young, but regional differences have to be considered. The youngest Christian populations are in sub-Saharan Africa and Asia-Pacific. By contrast, the median ages of Christians in Europe and in North America are much higher.

Some observers have used these data to suggest that the youth of the global south will determine the interests of the Church of the future. One problem with such a claim is that the religious lives of young people in Latin America, Asia, and Africa are not homogeneous. In fact, the youth in the global north cannot be essentialized either. The liberal-conservative stereotype about the north-south divide is inadequate in capturing the complex religious lives of young people today.

Such complexity is revealed when one considers what is at stake for the Church: abortion, same-sex marriage, cohabitation, divorce, celibacy, and the leadership of women and LGBT. In discussing each of these issues, context matters especially because religious and moral dispositions are shaped by the broader social environment, which, apart from age, includes ethnicity, class, geography, and denomination. My goal in this discussion will thus be modest. Two issues are explored here: changing religiosities and changing moral views.

In terms of changing religiosities, a pattern is discernible in the West, especially in North America: the rise of the religiously unaffiliated. In fact, in 2015, 35% of Americans below 30 years old did not have any religious affiliation. This figure increased faster than researchers anticipated. What is interesting about these 'Nones', as they are called in the literature, is that they are not militant atheists. They have their own spiritual practices – including prayer – that draw inspiration from different traditions and philosophies. An intriguing fact: 70% were raised in religiously affiliated families, most of whom are Christian.[12] But such spiritual explorations are not necessarily unique to American youth. My own work on Filipino Catholic youth shows that they, too, are flexible about their religious convictions and practices.[13] Although they consider themselves Catholic, they draw inspiration from various religious resources. In addition, many of them may not attend Mass regularly but are active in community engagements where they find religious meanings. While these Catholics have a clear religious affiliation and Nones do not, these two groups share discernible commonalities. Whereas Nones are choosing their religion, the Catholics I interviewed are reinterpreting religion in ways that make it meaningful on their own terms. Their case complicates the stereotype that Christianity in the global south is by default pious and conservative.

How moral world views are changing for the Church's youth around the world is also complex. I have mentioned a few controversial issues above. But for the sake of discussion, same-sex marriage is worth considering because it grabs the attention of Christians and non-Christians alike. The global divide over this issue is typically associated with economic advancement. Rich welfare states have legalized same-sex marriage, setting the international norm for developing countries. But a generational pattern is also noticeable. Young people in North America, Australia, and western Europe are more open to same-sex marriage than adults. Is the same pattern discernible elsewhere? The general trend might be that Catholic and Protestant groups outside the West maintain their resistance to same-sex marriage. Nevertheless, it is noteworthy that there are now LGBT-friendly Christian communities in such places as Singapore, Hong Kong,

Thailand, Mexico, and even Nigeria. These communities are attracting young people who consider themselves affirming and open-minded. They might constitute only a minority at this point but their situation is indicative of the shape of the Church of the future. Same-sex marriage and other related concerns such as the appointment of LGBT leaders in Christian communities will be a battleground as the international norm is set in place by legal structures. Young people are very much part of these tensions.

(b) Global inequality

The other challenge that the Church of the future faces is global inequality. In spite of the World Bank's goal of shared prosperity for all, social realities point to a different future: the ageing of developed societies, the emergence of new geopolitical conflicts, the fractures of the welfare system, and the rise of right-wing politics and violent extremism are all tied to social inequality or disparities in income and access to basic goods and services. Attempts to address inequality through science and technology are welcome but far too often they benefit the affluent first. In addition, the world's poor are most vulnerable to disasters and climate change that exacerbate inequality.[14] There is no sign that any of these problems will fade out soon.

How is global inequality affecting the Church though? The answer lies in what it means to be Church. One understanding is to associate Church with global social action. Churches in developed countries have been involved in addressing inequality around the world. Their missions are often accompanied by humanitarian work. There are also Christian humanitarian organizations such as Catholic Relief Services and World Vision. They are part of the global tapestry of the Church. But at the door of the Church in the West are many glaring instances of global inequality, chief of which is the concern about immigrants and refugees. Some Christian groups have been on the defensive, while others have been very responsive. The Church is very much implicated in politics of inclusion and exclusion.

Theological discourses are another example for how global inequality affects the Church. The growth of Christianity among the poor in developing countries might explain some shifts in theology. Liberation

43

theology may have generally weakened in the wake of neoliberalism but there are permutations in relation to specific issues. Parishes and faith-based organizations draw inspiration from Catholic Social Teaching, for example, to bring back human dignity to global debates about climate change and epidemics. But it needs to be emphasized that the global south is not all poor. The expansion of the middle class has paved the way for a self-driven theology that focuses on salvation, spiritual growth, and character to frame such biblical concepts as discipleship and calling. In some cases, this theology comes close to prosperity preaching. In contrast to their activist counterparts, such communities, however, are not necessarily political. The extent of their political involvement, as in the case of megachurches in Singapore, has to do with the defence of the heteronormative family. In Hong Kong, many Christian leaders have distanced themselves from democratic protests led by the youth.

I end this section by connecting global inequality and generational shifts. Presenting a coherent picture of what the Church does in relation to these issues is impossible because local contexts still matter. As the examples above show, some patterns are glaring, while others are still emerging. The crucial point is that uniformity is not to be expected from the Church of the future. One reason is that there are hot-button issues that will continue to divide Christian communities and individuals. Same-sex marriage and attitudes to prosperity are two significant examples.

At the centre of these developments are the youth and what religion means to them. Young people deserve attention not only because the Church is relatively young in terms of demographics but also because they are the leaders of the Church of the future. Will they still be around? Indeed, within their group we find greater flexibility towards religious beliefs, practices, and even affiliation. Theirs is an ethos that owes much to personal experience and an ongoing search for authenticity. This means that the hierarchy of the Church and its promulgations do not immediately earn their respect or submission. Unfortunately, it does not help that the hierarchy has to face numerous accusations of patriarchy, clericalism, and even corruption.

Young people are also at the centre of global inequality. While there are those who are enjoying the prosperity of economic growth in some parts of the world, many others are disenfranchised not by choice but by heightened vulnerabilities. The illustrations above have shown that inequality exists not only between but also within countries. These experiences colour young people's response to the Church, which can either draw from its resources to respond or simply back off.

The realization here is that whatever the Church does or does not do can spell the extent of its relevance to today's youth. In this light, the Church of the future is an achievement because it first depends on what the Church does now in relation to its future leaders. But at the same time the Church of the future rests on whether young people themselves find inspiration from its resources in the here and now.

IV Conclusion

This paper began by spelling out the global character of the Church. The prediction that Christianity will move to a specific region is not consistent with the state of affairs. It is one thing to rely on statistical data. But statistical data betray the otherwise rich engagements that the Church as a network of congregations, parishes, missions, and movements is accomplishing around the world. What this shows is that inasmuch as the demographic profile of the typical Christian may be changing, the Church's incarnation in other parts of the world has not fizzled out. The character of the Church of the future is tied to the complex processes of globalization.

It does not mean, however, that the future of the Church is secure with global society. On the contrary, it needs to establish its position again and again. This is because the most pervasive systems of global society have a tendency to marginalize religion. The global and secular systems of capitalism, international relations, and the scientific enterprise have taken over much of the conventional tasks of religion in welfare, education, and even everyday life. In this light, the active networks discussed above are performative attempts by the Church to assert its presence as a worthwhile institution in contemporary global society.[15] It has successfully created communities and fostered new identities. The Church of the future needs to imagine how it can continue to take advantage of these networks to sense and address global challenges. Young people are implicated in however the Church chooses to respond.

The sociological analysis that underpins this paper aligns with how Pope

Jayeel Cornelio

Francis understands the world today as a polyhedron, a community of many identities. In his view, the globalization of the Church must be reworked not as a mode of colonization from the centre that homogenizes every place it reaches. The Church of the future can benefit from a polyhedral perspective. It recognizes many modes of differences that are not only cultural. This article has framed these differences in terms of generational shifts and global inequality. These challenges demand humility from those who constitute the Church of today. Such an attitude resists the arrogance of a triumphalist eschatology. The Church of the future is contingent upon the Church of today that listens and responds to the world it inhabits.

Notes

1. Pew Research, *The Future of World Religions: Population Growth Projections*, 2010-2050, Pew Research Center, 2015, p. 231.
2. H. Cox, 'Thinking globally about Christianity', in M. Juergensmeyer (ed.) *The Oxford Handbook of Global Religions*, Oxford and NY: Oxford University Press, 2006, p. 245.
3, C. Selin, 'The Sociology of the Future: Tracing Stories of Technology and Time', *Sociology Compass* 6 (2008), p. 1885.
4. J. Beckford, 'Globalisation and Religion', in V. Altglas (ed.) *Religion and Globalization: Critical Concepts in Social Studies*, vol. 3, London and NY: Routledge, 2011, p. 46.
5. P. Beyer, *Religion and Globalization*, London: Sage, 1994, p. 71.
6. P. Jenkins, *The Next Christendom: The Coming of Global Christianity*, 3rd ed., Oxford: Oxford University Press, 2011, p. xi.
7. Pew Research, T*he Changing Global Religious Landsape*, Pew Research Center, 2017, pp. 10, 29.
8. J. Beckford, 2011, p. 5.
9. J. Beckford, 2011, p. 5.
10. H. Cox, 2006, p. 252.
11. Pew Research, 2015, p. 66.
12. E. Drescher, *Choosing Our Religion: The Spiritual Lives of America's Nones*, New York: Oxford University Press, 2016, p. 8.
13. J. Cornelio, *Being Catholic in the Contemporary Philippines: Young People Reinterpreting Religion*, London and New York: Routledge, 2016, p. 76.
14. J. Urry, *Climate Change and Society*, Cambridge and Malden, MA: Polity, 2011, p. 6.
15. P. Beyer, 1994, pp. 71-72.

The 'Tensions' in the Church Today: Four Fundamental Challenges

VIRGINIA R. AZCUY

The perspective of 'practical ecclesiology' may help us to imagine the Church of the future starting from the real Church we are, holy and sinful. Because of its historical nature, the Church community is in tension between its present, sometimes contradictory, reality and the hope springing up from its own desires for reform. The call to life in abundance demands the humility to face failure and limitation. A consideration of the Church in terms of practical theology could be expressed by four fundamental challenges: low credibility, the deformation of clericalism, a male bias and spiritual worldliness. The article tries to focus some key questions that need to be addressed if we are to discern what Church we want.

The Church that journeys in history towards the kingdom of God is 'in tension' between its pilgrim state and its eschatological goal, between its scandals and its aspirations to reform. This text is not about the ideal of perfect Church that we are called to be in plenitude, but about the real Church, holy and sinful, that we are in the present. The 'practical ecclesiology' approach may help us to rethink the Church as it is and dream of the future because it points us to a theology of the Church in dialogue with experiences of the Church.[1] Its attempt to look closely at this Church looks at the imperfect holiness of the body of Christ in order above all to discover the temptations and weaknesses that slow its mission, without of course forgetting the signs of its growing holiness. Looking from this perspective, what I want to do is to consider in theological terms the empirical reality of the Church with regard to four fundamental challenges:

the crisis of credibility, crippling clericalism, the male bias and spiritual worldliness. These challenges produce a tension in the Church around the various proposals for renewal and *aggiornamento*, which I shall try to outline briefly, together with some possible theological analyses.

I A Church with a credibility crisis or the challenge of public scrutiny

In an information society, and one shaken by various cases of corruption and new standards of transparency in public affairs, the Catholic Church in Chile is in the throes of a crisis of confidence with no historic precedent. The case of Chile, which is emblematic for South America, can serve us as a reference point for analysing the new demands for accountability that the Church needs to accept. According to the *Latinobarómetro* poll, only one in three Chileans trusts the institutional Church as a result of the abuse scandals: trust fell from 80% to 36%. It was hoped that Pope Francis' visit to the country between 15 and 18 January 2018 could be a catalyst for a resolution of the crisis and allow for a new start. The Pope had to face at least three delicate issues: the impact of the sexual abuses committed by bishops, priests and religious of the Catholic Church, the historic issue of the first peoples as illustrated by the Mapuche land conflict, and the conflict between Chile and Bolivia over Bolivian access to the Pacific. The official programme started on Tuesday 16 January with a message delivered by the Pope in the presidential palace of La Moneda, in which the most striking point was the apology for the cases of sexual abuse:

> I cannot fail to display the *pain and shame* I feel for the irreparable harm done to children by ministers of the Church. It is right to ask for forgiveness and to do all that we can to support the victims, and at the same time to make every effort to ensure that this does not happen again.

This mea culpa on the part of Francis, who insists that he has 'zero tolerance' in this area, won support from public opinion and established a standard or threshold for other Church authorities, as the Catholic theologian Claudia Leal has pointed out.

The bishop of Rome's bold declaration in La Moneda proved

insufficient shortly afterwards as a result of the scandal caused by the presence of Bishop Juan Barros at activities that were part of the official programme. Barros had been accused of covering up the sexual crimes of the priest Fernando Karadima, who was convicted in 2010, and his appointment as bishop of Osorno in 2015 was greeted with suspicion and protests, which revived with his public appearance at ceremonies presided over by Francis. The most common reactions were criticism on social media, anger on the part of the victims and dismay on the part of many Catholics. The tension reached a peak on Thursday 18 January in Iquique, when, in a brief remark to the press, the pope claimed he 'had no evidence' against Barros, giving the impression that he was defending the bishop and discrediting the victims. Why was it not possible to avoid this new public 'exposure' of the Catholic Church, which increased its lack of credibility? The well-known sociologist of religion, Cristián Parker, discussed the 'transparency' required today by technological societies.[2] He maintained that in the Karadima case the 'passive accomplices' had not been considered, that is, those who had not reported his crimes although they had witnessed or been close to them.[2a]

In other contexts, the situation is not very different as regards the crisis of credibility and public relevance of the Church. Witness – personal, communal and institutional – continues to be a decisive mediation for the transmission of the faith in today's situation. In the face of situations of sexual abuse on the part of its members, the Church is called to listen to the victims, investigate the facts and identify the guilty, use the necessary resources to secure justice, publicly apologise and commit to prevention. It is true that important steps in this direction have been taken, but much remains to be done to take further the reform the Catholic Church needs. As the Second Vatican Council taught, the Church is 'at the same time holy and always in need of purification...day by day' (*Lumen Gentium* 8; *Unitatis redintegratio* 4,4). Reform of the Church and reforms in the Church have already started but need to be taken still further; they must be in the service of a pastoral ministry appropriate to our time and one that meets the legitimate demands of civil society. 'Anyone thinking today about the reform of the Church cannot fail to analyse the world and society as they are today, as the Council did.'[3] In a society dominated by new information technologies, where new standards of truth apply in social affairs, the Church needs to continue growing in the public dimension of its vocation so that the Gospel and be seen more completely and better understood (*Gaudium et spes*, 44). To achieve this pastoral approach adequate to our time, we need not just to proclaim but also to listen to the Gospel, the history of our time and every Christian. What actions is the Church called on to take to ensure that the force of the Spirit can freely be revealed in itself? How could she reform herself to be a better mediator of justice, mercy, reconciliation and forgiveness?

II A Church deformed by clericalism – or the prophecy of being sisters and brothers

The issue of sexual abuses in the Church and inadequate institutional responses reveals a complex structural picture. As shown by the Final Report of the Australian Royal Commission into Institutional Responses to Child Sexual Abuse, 'a combination of cultural, governance and theological factors' are among those that contribute to the sexual abuse of children. In the Catholic Church institutions examined by the commission, 'the central factor, underpinning and linked to all other factors, was the status of people in religious ministry'. The report notes that this factor, 'described in some contexts as "clericalism"', contributed both to the occurrence of abuse and to the inadequate responses.[4] The commission's recommendations focus on the factors that facilitate abuse and the inadequate institutional responses, including the religious beliefs and practices that may favour the repetition of these crimes. In view of the structural character and the moral seriousness of the problem of abuse, it is appropriate to turn our attention to the theology of the Church and the place of the hierarchy.

The Second Vatican Council revised ecclesiology and suggested moving from a hierarchical vision to a communitarian one. Its contribution was to recover the patristic ecclesiology in which the Church was seen as a *communio* of believers and churches, certainly a corrective to a hierarchical and centralised vision. In the practical process of renewal, the priority given to the people of God vis à vis the hierarchy turned out to be more difficult and slower to implement than expected. If the Church is first and foremost *plebs adunata*. 'A people united as one in the unity of the triune God' (LG 4), the mystery of the Trinity is the foundation of ecclesial communion: the Church shares the unity of God who is Father. Son and Holy Spirit. But, as H. Legrand notes, the primary task of Vatican II was not to develop the topic of the 'synodal' or journeying together (*syn-odos*) character of the Church, but the relations between the papacy and the bishops. Medard Kehl argues that unequal weight is given to the hierarchical and synodal principles of the Church, although both belong to its basic structure; he also points out that a theology of communion that is not translated into structures is simply irrelevant. Accordingly, there is still an important task outstanding: 'This renewed synodal ecclesiology demands to be implemented in tangible ways; in the Church and the particular churches it calls in question all individuals and all structures at all levels, local, national, regional and global.'[5] The logical implication of this argument would be to explore the various issues and bodies in the catholic Church open to *synodal* reform, but instead I shall discuss a much more limited and sensitive discussion on the *excessive clericalism which keeps them out of decision-making* (*Evangelii Gaudium*, 102). What could be prompting Francis to keep stressing this issue? Perhaps it is the fact that clericalism as an expression of the superiority of the clerical state to other vocations is an obstacle to the building up of the Church as the body of Christ and disregards the dignity of the weaker members of the faithful people (1 Cor 12.4-26).

Theologians from all over the world, brought together by the International Federation of Catholic Universities (FIUC) for the 50th anniversary of Vatican II, reminded us of the relational character of the Church, which needs the charisms of each and every one of its members if it is to carry out its mission. The challenge seems to lie in constantly looking for ways to enable the whole of Christian existence to bear fruit for the people of God as a whole in the service of humanity. Dialogue between the different ways of life and their mutual collaboration turns out to be *par excellence* the way to be Church; while there are many examples of this, there is room to move forward with management strategies to ensure a harmonious interaction between charism and authority. There is a need for comradeship or cooperation between priests, those in consecrated life and lay people to perfect forms of exercising power, authority and leadership that are shared. What can each vocation contribute? How should we evaluate the task of presbyters to discern the signs of the times alongside the laity? What is there to say about the lay apostolate, derived from the laity's own union with Christ the Head? How far can consecrated life and married life make their own specific prophetic contribution for the whole Church to strengthen the 'mutual relations' between the different forms of Christian life (PO 9; AA 3; MR 15ff)? In the different ways in which the presbyterate, consecrated life and laity can exchange experiences, meet and enrich each other, we can begin to see a style of Church life that is more synodal. The temptation of clericalism undermines the best intentions of dialogue, collaboration and recognition; working in a synodal way requires adequate structures and a spirituality of mutual service. If we manage to understand and out into practice the truth that the common priesthood of the faithful and the ministerial priesthood 'are interrelated' (LG 10), it then begins to be possible to make the one people a reality. Only if we succeed in creating a community of equals – through baptism – with a diversity of charisms and ministries, can we proclaim the prophecy of a community or body of sisters and brothers around Jesus.[6] This prophecy of life as a family has already come true in many marriages, in communities of consecrated life and team ministries, in many parish and diocesan communities, but it still needs to be purified and grow more strongly.

III A Church with a male bias – or the hope of an inclusive community

Fifty years after the Second Vatican Council it is reasonable to ask if the issue of women as a sign of the times has been taken seriously. The majority of textbooks or articles on ecclesiology available in Spanish continue to ignore the question of women and a gender perspective when dealing with the Church, although it is an issue dealt with in papal teaching and theological research – especially in feminist theology – for decades now. As Margit Eckholt and Massimo Faggioli, among others, note, the contributions of women theologians on the question of the reception of Vatican II ecclesiology have been more or less ignored. What can explain this omission? Can the Church and academic community ignore this issue? The male bias the Catholic Church displays, even though women make up the majority of its members, really is a red-hot issue for the transmission of the faith in our time.

In 1963, at the end of the third session of Vatican II, Cardinal Leon Joseph Suenens suggested the inclusion of women as 'auditors' or guests at the Council, a practice without precedent in the history of Church councils. He did so in a public intervention on the charismatic dimension of the Church in which he referred to the fundamental importance of charisms in the construction of the mystical body and the need to avoid the impression that the hierarchical Church was an administrative apparatus disconnected from them. Marinella Perroni interpreted the position of the archbishop of Mechelen-Brussels as the beginning of 'the abandonment of an ecclesiology that discriminated by gender' because it integrated the charismatic dimension alongside the hierarchical in the people of God and, slowly, opened the way to an inclusive ecclesiology. In the ecclesiology of *Lumen Gentium* the topic was explored in Chapter IV, on the laity, within the framework of the one people of God, formed by different members united by *one Lord, one faith, one baptism* (cf Eph 4.5). One example is the second paragraph of section 32, which states that the members of the people of God have the same dignity and the same grace by being children of God and that there is therefore no inequality by reason of race, sex or social condition, and refers to Gal 3.28 and Col 3.11. The *nulla inaequalitas* ('no inequality') is irrefutable: in the Church there can be no question of discrimination of any kind. The Italian theologian Cettina Militello says that the main point is how to develop the teachings of LG 10-12: the challenge for today is 'to translate the baptismal subjectivity [of women] into all possible forms, receiving and developing the Council debate'.[7] To carry out *diakonia*, ministry and service in the Church, the Spirit needs anointed human protagonists, men and women.

As theologians from all over the world, men and women, recognise, women play a fundamental role in the Church's pastoral work. In many regions they are the majority of the lay ministers that serve in parishes or diocesan bodies as catechists, teachers, canonists and administrators. The theological community includes competent women who make notable contributions in different areas, but their contributions are not always recognized and valued in the Church. We need to continue our journey towards women's full participation in the Church community, especially in decision-making.

Speaking from her specialist field of canon law, the German theologian

Sabine Demel talks about women's ministries not only as a debt owed by the Church, but also as a 'theological debt' because she finds an omission:

'The issue of women in the Church cannot be a *pragmatic* decision, but has to be a fundamental theological decision: we have to express, ultimately, that the Church needs women, and needs them as partners of equal status – not because otherwise it would have fewer staff to carry out everyday tasks and would have to change its mission, but because it is an issue of the image and likeness of the human being as male and female. The image and likeness and the reciprocity of man and woman has nothing to do with a gender hierarchy that does not derive from Jesus and is not redeemed.'[8]

This brings up a core theological idea, one explored by the Norwegian woman Catholic theologian Kari Borresen: man and woman as the image of God. Part of Demel's analysis that it would be timely to pick up is what she says about the female diaconate, which she suggests would be a challenge for our time.

IV A worldly Church – or the spiritual art of 'stereophonic listening'

The Church becomes worldly when it loses the perspective of the kingdom of God and his righteousness, as the Salvadorean martyr Ignacio Ellacuría put it. Worldliness grows in the churches, among other reasons, through the lack of a spirituality capable of listening; the fundamental mediations of the encounter with God fail and the Spirit is prevented from moving those who wish to follow Jesus. For Francis, 'Spiritual worldliness, which hides behind the appearance of piety and even love for the Church, consists in seeking not the Lord's glory but human glory and personal well-being' (*Evangelii Gaudium*, 93). To avoid it, or cure it, a key piece of advice is to press for an 'outgoing' Church, devoted to Jesus Christ in service of the poor and of the Spirit who frees us from every appearance of religion that is empty of God. The worldliness of the Church can be overcome by 'stereophonic listening', which helps us to go out from ourselves and receive simultaneously the Word in the scriptures and in the cry of the poor and of the earth.[9]

The first place for this listening is the World of God in the bible, since 'ignorance of scripture is ignorance of Christ', as *Dei Verbum*, 25 reminds us in the words of St Jerome, and this listening is recommended in liturgical celebrations by *Sacrosanctum Concilium*, 35. The practice of a prayerful reading of the bible, already present in the bible itself and described systematically by the medieval monk Guigo II, the Carthusian, teaches us to follow the recommendation of Ps 95.7: 'O that today you would listen to his voice!' In recent decades *lectio divina* has gone beyond the personal sphere and become a central element of diocesan pastoral ministry, an ordinary pastoral tool that guides Christian commitment in everyday life. In Latin America since the 1960s, the main innovation in the Church is represented by the rediscovery of the Word of God by the poor. Carlos Mesters has said: 'A holy and prayerful life cannot be lived to the full if we do not feel the need for the prayerful reading of the bible.'10 The practice of lectio points the path to holiness, not only for monastic and other forms of consecrated life (PC 6; VC 112), but for the whole Church, which is called to listen to, welcome and proclaim the Word (DV 10).

The listening is extended into history as a community discernment of the signs of the times: God speaks in the bible and in the present time through the power of the Spirit. Vatican II offers a model of a Church that learns from history so that it can proclaim the Gospel in a way that it can be better understood and accepted (GS 44). The Church of Latin America and the Caribbean has contributed to explain the importance of listening to the cry for justice. As the place where Christ is present, the poor and the victims – women and children, indigenous people, migrants and others – constitute a fundamental path of faith: *closing our ears to the cry of the poor and the victims is to close our ears to Christ, who, though he was rich, became poor and a victim* (cf 2 Cor 8.9). Pope Francis recognizes the importance of going out from oneself to others as the criterion of any moral rule or test of discernment of spiritual growth (EG 179). Spiritual worldliness represents a flight from the world or an attempt to escape from history, but a contemplative listening to the cry of the poor and the cry of the earth helps us to tune into the Spirit. The martyr's witness of Sister Dorothy Stang in her peaceful fight against the illegal deforestation of the jungle and the exploitation of the rural workers can be seen as a real-life example of the spiritual skill of stereophonic listening. She was attacked as she walked to a meeting of small farmers near Anapu in Brazil's Amazon region. Her pursuers asked her if she was armed and she took out the bible she carried in her bag and began to read from the beatitudes: 'Blessed are the peacemakers, for they will be called children of God' (Mt 5.9). With these words she gave her life for the kingdom and its justice, when one of her attackers fired three shots and killed her, on 12 February 2005.

V Some theological conclusions
The real Church, which is endowed with an imperfect holiness and is called to permanent renewal, displays a tension between its weaknesses and its strengths. Called to be a *sacrament of salvation in history*, it needs to recognize that it is under public scrutiny and faces the challenge of being a witness capable of inspiring credibility. Our present-day societies can contribute to the processes of sanctification and reform of the churches by exposing their contradictions and calling for greater coherence between their words and their actions. In dialogue with surrounding society, the Church can discover the guidance it needs to identify specific aspects of the reform it is called on to carry out; this contribution it receives from contemporary history, united always to the inspiration of revelation, may be a unique opportunity for learning and *aggiornamento*.

Called to live in *communion* as the people of God, the body of Christ and the temple of the Spirit, the pilgrim Church must feel herself driven to overcome the worrying ecclesiological deformation that is clericalism, which inevitably favours abuse of power and hinders the practice of *synodality*. Only the experience of life as a *family of disciples* – with different forms of Christian life, races and cultures – can be worthy of faith. Recognition of difference and comradeship in the Church between the different vocation, charisms and ministries could be new names for communion. After all, how can a Church with a male bias effectively proclaim redemption to women, men, girls and boys of the 21st century? The equal baptismal dignity of every Christian must be translated into Church services and ministries, into new and creative synodal forms of participation, discernment and decision-making. The path of theology and practice calls for a pastoral, structural conversion that moves from an ecclesiology that still discriminates to one that is increasingly inclusive.

Finally, a Church that allows itself to be placed under tension by its vocation for the kingdom must find effective mediations for a stereophonic spirituality if it is to discern and act according to its discernment. Without the action of the Spirit there is no way that the coming together of believers can be an eschatological sign for a humanity that is broken, weakened and in search of meaning. In listening to the Word that can be heard in scripture and in our time, if we avoid the temptation of spiritual worldliness and increasingly seek dialogue with others, the community of all the baptised can allow itself to be taken to a fuller, final future. The witness of the saints and martyrs of today can point the way ahead.

Translated by Francis McDonagh

Virginia R. Azcuy

Notes

Abbreviations for documents of the Second Vatican Council
AA: Decree on the Apostolate of the Laity (*Apostolicam actuositatem* PC: Decree on the Renewal of the Religious Life (*Perfectae caritatis*)

1. Cf. N. M. Healy, *Church, World and the Christian Life: Practical-Prophetic Ecclesiology*, Cambridge, 2000; P. Ward (ed.), *Perspectives on Ecclesiology and Ethnography*, Grand Rapids, Michigan/Cambridge, U.K., 2012.

2. Cf. C. Parker, 'El Obispo Barros y la transparencia': http://www.elmostrador.cl/%20 noticias/opinion/2018/01/24/el-obispo-barros-y-la-transparencia / (accessed: 23.07.2018).

2a. After the protests that greeted his defence of Bishop Barros during his visit in January 2018, Pope Francis sent an experienced investigator, Archbishop Charles Sicluna, to Chile, though when Sicluna fell ill the investigation was carried out by his assistant, Fr Jordi Bartolomeu. After receiving the report, the Pope invited three of the victims to Rome, where they had a friendly meeting, and summoned the Chilean bishops to a meeting in Rome in May, At the end of the meeting, on 18 May, in an unprecedented move, the Chilean bishops offered their resignations *en masse*. By the end of June the Pope had accepted the renunciations of five of them, including Barros. See Austen Ivereigh,'A Church in denial', *The Tablet*, 5 May 2018, 4-5 (*Translator's note*).

3. H. J. Pottmeyer, 'La Iglesia en camino para configurarse como Pueblo de Dios', in: A. Spadaro and C. M. Galli (ed.), *La reforma y las reformas en la Iglesia*, Santander, 2016, pp 79-93, esp. 79 and 84.

4. Cf. *Royal Commission into Institutional Responses to Child Sexual Abuse, Final Report*, Vol. 16: *Religious Institutions* (Books 1-3), Commonwealth of Australia, 2017, Book 1, p. 28: https://www.childabuseroyalcommission.gov.au/sites/default/files/final_ report_-_ volume_16_religious_ institutions_book_1.pdf (accessed 23.07.18).

5. C. Schickendantz, 'Sinodalidad en todos los niveles: Teología, diagnóstico y propuestas para una reforma institucional', in: V. R. Azcuy, J. C. Caamaño and C. M. Galli (ed.), *La Eclesiología del Concilio Vaticano II: Memoria, Reforma y Profecía*, Buenos Aires, 2015, pp 513-534, quotation p. 518.

6. Cf S. M. Schneiders, 'La vida religiosa en el futuro', in: U*nión de Superiores Generales – Unión Internacional de Superioras Generales, Pasión por Cristo, pasión por la humanidad*, Madrid, 2005, 3rd reprint 2006, pp 229-273, esp. pp 247-248. (English edition: *International Congress on Consecrated Life, Passion of Christ, passion for humanity*, Boston MA, 2005).

7. C. Militello, 'Le donne e la riscoperta della dignità battismale', in: M. Perroni, A. Melloni and S. Noceti (ed.), *"Tantum aurora est": Donne e Concilio Vaticano II*, Zürich and Berlin, 2012, pp 219-254, quotation p. 242.

8. S. Demel, *Frauen und kirchliches Amt: Grundlagen-Grenzen-Möglichkeiten*, Freiburg-Basle-Vienna, 2012, p. 16.

9. Cf. Ch. Theobald, 'Paroles humaines – Parole de Dieu : Quelques réflections théologiques et pastorales à partir de la constitution Dei Verbum de Vatican II', *Cahiers Évangile* 175 (2016), 38-52; G. Söding, 'Una escucha "estereofónica": El Texto y la Vida interpretan la Palabra', in: V. R. Azcuy, D. García and C. Schickendantz (eds), *Lugares e interpelaciones de Dios: Discernir los signos de los tiempos*, Santiago, 2017, pp 71-104.

10. C. Mesters, *Hacer arder el corazón: Introducción a la lectura orante de la Palabra*, Estella, 2006, pp 15-16.

The Church of the Future in Africa: A Path to the Praxis of Pope Francis's Illuminative Ecclesiology in African Catholicism

STAN CHU ILO

This essay looks at what the Church of the future in Africa could look like in the light the missionary reform of Catholic ecclesiology in Pope Francis. It also explores what World Catholicism will look like in such a future where African Catholics and churches are playing a significant role in shape the identity and mission of the Universal Church. Using the illuminative ecclesiology of Pope Francis as a guide, the essay looks at the present challenges and features of the Church in Africa. The essay concludes by laying the theological foundation of a roadmap for the Church in Africa. Such a Church, it will be shown will be an agent in reversing the unacceptable trajectory of history in the continent by being a poor and merciful Church fully involved in the mission of bringing about the fruits of the eschatological reign of God in both Africa and the world.

I Introduction

This essay imagines the future of the Church in Africa using the reform of Catholic ecclesiology in Pope Francis as a guide. It identifies the signs of the times in the Christian mission in Africa and the strengths and weaknesses of emerging paradigms of Church life in Africa today. It proposes five steps towards the Church of the future in Africa and how the African continent will look like when it is served by a poor and merciful Church which embraces the praxis of illuminative ecclesiology.

II The Church of Pope Francis and the theological aesthetics of illuminative ecclesiology

I have argued in a recent book that Pope Francis has introduced a new ecclesiological paradigm today through the theological aesthetics of a poor and merciful Church.[1] This paradigm focuses not on *who* the Church is but on *where* the Church is. The mission of the Church is to illuminate the lives of people with words and deeds modelled after the example of the Lord Jesus.[2] The Church can bring the light of Christ to all people (*Lumen Gentium* [LG] 1) only by both being close to the Lord and to God's people, especially the poor and the wounded, in their daily joys and sorrows. The Church exists to bring about a closer following of the Lord through meeting people with the logic of love and mercy at the multiple sites of human experiences, especially in 'those unconventional modes of beauty' (*Evangelii Gaudium* [EG] 167, see also EG 168–169).

This new paradigm is an *ecclesiology of accountability* which renders praise to God by showing how the Church can be open to the diverse gifts of humanity and creation as sources of divine light in the world. It is an *ecclesiology of accompaniment* because it shows how the Church, through her sacraments, ecclesial life, ministries, structures, laws and relationships, can become a travelling companion to all the people of God through a missional praxis which proceeds through a vulnerable mission. It is an *ecclesiology of action* because it constantly examines the inner and external life of the Church in order to develop a relevant daily praxis which brings about ongoing conversion, healing and transformation of the people of God, the Church, society and creation so that the eschatological fruits of God's kingdom can be more fully realized in history.

Pope Francis is calling the Church today to move away from an enslavement to structures and systems to a missionary reform of the Church wherein all her actions, laws, pastoral actions and relationships are driven by 'the delightful and comforting joy of evangelization' (EG 14–18). This can come about through a Church which 'goes forth' as a 'community of missionary disciples' to generously and boldly offer the mercy of God to the people of God, especially the outcasts (EG 24). At the core of the new ecclesiological paradigm of Pope Francis is the missionary conversion to which he calls the Church. This begins not from an essentialized notion of

Church or of doctrine and self-assertions but rather from the experience of marginality of all humanity and creation in our poverty and sin where we are most in need of God's mercy and love (EG15, 17, 25, 119–121).[3]

This emphasis on encountering people and bringing light into the lives of people and finding light in the most obscure places is at the heart of the aesthetics of this theology of Church which I have termed an illuminative ecclesiology. This is an ecclesiology which answers the question: what form of witnessing and proclamation should be found in our Churches, among Christians and Church ministers, which shows the merciful, tender and loving face of God to the world and brings the diverse faces and conditions of all of God's people to God? I argue that in Pope Francis's priorities and practices, which show the portrait of the Church as poor and merciful, we have indications of how the faces of all of God's people can be reflected as in a mirror to God and how God can encounter all people, and use the gifts of all people in the Church. This theological aesthetics points to how the light of Christ is mediated in concrete human and cosmic experience and shows how our human condition is shot through with a hidden illumination which the Church can only discover through her encounter with the 'other.'

The core of the theological aesthetics of illuminative ecclesiology is the love of God, which is encountered as first love and internal word of life in every instance of encounter with the other, especially in the experience of human brokenness. The Lord is present in every human and cosmic reality. This is an incomparable incarnational moment. The Lord has promised to be present in the Church and in history, especially in the life and reality of the least of the brothers and sisters. The answer then to the question 'Where is the Church?' is always to be found in the portrait of the everyday experiences of humanity and the world as touched by the hand of a loving and merciful God through the instrumentality of the Church and her members. The love of God the Father is revealed to all Christians and the Church in the midst of sins, wounds and brokenness and can be experienced as a saving light in the humble obedience and attunement of the Church to her Trinitarian origin and model.

The first truth for Christians, according to Pope Francis, is not a name¬less being or truth, but a truth that has a wounded face, Jesus Christ. This incarnate love – the light of the world in the Church and in history

– is prior to and the foundation and source of all being and all things that the Church teaches, professes and lives. This incarnate love, as Thomas Aquinas states, is an interior beauty as well as an interior grace (EG 37) which gives beauty to creation and defines the path of beauty for the Church. It is present in every instance of joy and pain of suffering humanity and the entire cosmos. Its presence in creation and in all of God's people becomes the primary identifier of where God is present and the sites of God's work in history of which the Church is a servant. Christian life is a vocation to embrace the 'way of beauty' (EG 167) even in the contradictions and complexities of life. The Church is called to walk the 'way of beauty' with humanity; this is an invitation to live in the truth by touching 'the human heart and enabling the truth and goodness of the Risen Christ to radiate within it' (EG 167).[4] The Church of the future must embrace the path of accountability, the art of accompaniment and a spiritual praxis of action through a vulnerable mission which brings integral salvation and transformation to a wounded world through memorialising in history the words and deeds of the Lamb that was slain.

III The signs of the times in Africa

There is a general consensus among Church historians and missiologists that the centre of gravity of World Catholicism is shifting to Africa and Latin America. This is evidenced in the exponential growth in the population of Catholics in the Churches of the Global South. What this means is that what is happening in these Churches may define the shape, identity and direction of the future of Catholicism in a post-Western Christianity and in post-Christian Western societies. It also means that these Churches should be given greater respect and autonomy in the Roman Catholic Church. This way, the gifts and dynamism of these Churches can flourish and their unique traditions and logics of belief and living can be used in addressing some of the contested questions about God, morality, marriage and spirituality (among others) which are highly divisive in today's World Church.

The Christian faith is alive and dynamic in Africa and the Churches in Africa are becoming strong drivers of social change. They are also increasingly visible agents and major players in all social, economic and political aspects of African societies. Indeed, one of the signs of the times in Africa is that Churches are acquiring strong social capital and providing interruptive agency to reverse the course of an unacceptable history in many social contexts in Africa where God's people are still nailed to the cross of poverty, suffering and misrule. In such marginal contexts, many Christians, especially women leaders and nuns, provide alternative sites of hope and belonging for women's groups and communities who are seeking a praxis of reversal through the agency of Churches. Catholic social ministries in the areas of education, agriculture, micro-credit, peace-building or healthcare have significant impact in many African societies.

However, despite all these positive signs, the Church in Africa faces mounting challenges. Some of the questions which many African Christians are asking as we move into the future are: What is the identity of the Churches of Africa? How are these Churches contributing to or hampering the emergence of the kind of future many Africans dream of for their societies? Can African types and models of Church become influential for the revival of the faith in the West if African Churches are still dependent financially on Western Churches? What images of the Church do African Christians embrace which could be seen as 'success stories' in dealing with the challenges of ethnocentric and clannish sentiments in African Churches? This also applies to instances of authoritarianism among some African Church leaders, the marginalization of women, and the highly clerical and cultic culture dominant in African Churches? What message will the Churches of Africa offer to World Christianity on how to deal with ecumenical and inter-faith relations? What are specific African Christian approaches to the religious persecution of Christians in some African countries with a predominant Muslim population, and how should Christianity relate to other cultural subjects, faith traditions and people on the margins in diverse societies in order to promote human and cosmic flourishing and the reign of God?

My contention here is that any realistic vision of the future of the Churches of Africa will require understanding the two contending narratives which define what has often been called the 'African predicament': the crisis of the post-colonial state in Africa and the crisis of post-missionary Christianity in Africa. These two crises give rise to contending cultural and socio-economic currents which are at play in Africa's search for her own version of modernity. These two crises can help to understand the cultural processes in religious narratives in Africa with regard to the exponential growth in the Christian population in the continent, the rise in African Pentecostal and Charismatic movements, the challenges and limitations of political and religious leadership in Africa, religious fragmentation and religious competition; as well as the permeable and multiple religious loyalties and the persistence of cultic clericalism and the patriarchal marginalization of women in African Catholicism and more widely, in African societies.

These are also key for interpreting the challenging socio-economic conditions under which the majority of Africans live which are determining the life outcomes for millions of people. All these are emerging as people, ethnic and religious groups form social, religious and political alignments in the competition for power and interests to meet the perceived deprivation which arises from the inchoate social compact in most African countries amidst the spectre of poverty and structural violence. This is the bigger picture through which one can read both the so-called religious extremism in some parts of Africa, as well as the migration and humanitarian crisis which face millions of Africans in many parts of the continent. It can also help us to understand questions about poverty in Africa, the so-called prosperity gospel movements and the quest for healing and miracles in Churches.

IV The Church of Africa: A road map for the future

How can the Churches of Africa meet these challenges and opportunities amidst the exponential growth of the Christian faith in Africa? I propose five steps. The first is the development of a dynamic Catholic identity. Second, the development of a dynamic Catholic intellectual tradition. Third, the emergence of Catholic leadership which will help address the challenges facing the Church in Africa and influence the evolution of Churches in Africa in birthing African Christians who are strong in both manifestations of faith and works of faith. Fourth, addressing the social context of Africa where religion has become in many cases a means for problem-solving rather than a channel for intimate relationship with God, human beings and nature, a medium of integral salvation and human and cosmic flourishing. Fifth, the emergence of a true Catholicity in the wider Church which treats the Churches of Africa in the Catholic tradition as mature and adult Churches and not some ecclesial colonies dependent on the Church of Rome.

The first question relates to an ecclesiology of accountability, which gives praise to God for the gifts, which God has given to Africa. This is particularly with regard to the challenge of inculturating the Christian faith in Africa. The goal here is that the African who embraces the faith should find in it an integrative and coherent force for answering the myriad questions about what to believe, how to believe and how to live. Most scholars believe that the presence of a 'double conscience', 'schizoid faith', 'swinging faith' and 'permeable religious affinity' among many African Christians raise fundamental questions about the nature of conversion in African Christianity.[5] What are Africans converting from and what kind of faith and ecclesial life and structures are they embracing? What is the before and the after of conversion from African Traditional Religions (ATRs) to Christianity in Africa? This is particularly relevant with regard to the loose and experimental religious affinity in limit situations in the daily life and faith of many African Christians. This has given rise to a persistent culture-lag because the official faith of the Church in her teachings is sometimes at variance with the actual faith of African Christians and their internalized sources of validation and authentication of faith at the specific level of personal, cultural and communal self-understanding.

The Church of the future in Africa must work hard to realize the vision of the First African Synod on the urgency of inculturation in Africa in order to bridge the gulf between official and actual faith (Ecclesia in Africa 59). African Catholic bishops at the Synod also committed themselves to build the Church in Africa into self-sufficient communities of faith (EA 104) and to promote the cause of justice and peace (EA 112–114). This will require, as the First African Synod proposed, 'respecting, preserving and fostering the particular values and riches of Africa on one hand, while 'bringing Christ into the very centre of African life and of lifting African life to Christ' (EA 127).

The second challenge is that of the Catholic intellectual tradition. How are people socialized into the faith and how do African Catholics document models of faith, spirituality, morality or social ministries which are emerging features of the presence of the Church in Africa? What forms of Catholic life, spirituality and morality are emerging in Africa as a result of the presence of the Catholic Church which are transferable wisdom traditions which can help Africans to read the signs of the times? How do African Catholic scholars and pastors ground the understanding of Christian humanism, theological anthropology, Catholic social teaching among others through the Catholic heritage and vision as lived and celebrated in Africa today in conversation with Africa's rich intellectual and social justice traditions?

Deepening the faith in Africa will require the growth of the intellectual heritage of African Catholicism within the ever-expanding structure of the rich African intellectual heritage in dialogue with the enduring Catholic intellectual tradition. This entails a ceaseless search for how the Catholic faith – founded on the revealed truths of the Gospel and tradition – can be mediated through cultural knowledge, cultural artefacts and cultural behaviour autochthonous to Africa. I propose that this situation—the slow pace of the inculturation of the faith and the Gospel in Africa—should not be a source of grief but should be seen as signs that the Christian faith is going through a process of trial and formation in Africa. These are the painful birth pangs of a faith in transition from its missionary captivity to assuming its own voice, place and relevance in African religio-cultural and social history.

The third challenge is leadership. The recent crisis over the rejection of a bishop in Nigeria and the assassination of bishops in Cameroun and Kenya within the last few years all point to a troubling development in how ecclesial office and the exercise of authority in the Church are perceived. Some questions to be considered by the Church in Africa with regard to reforming the leadership in the local Churches in Africa are: How are leaders chosen in our Churches? Should the nuncios and officials in Rome be the ones who determine suitable candidates for episcopal offices, rectors of seminaries, heads of religious orders and Catholic social agencies in Africa? How do we raise future leaders in Africa through the Church? How do clerics and the religious exercise their offices in the Church in Africa? How credible and prophetic are the lifestyles of our Church leaders and the laity in various positions of leadership and what difference does their faith make in their witnessing to God through the positions which they occupy? The Church of the future in Africa must embrace a conscious and deliberate evangelical strategy for the leadership training and mentoring of the laity, the religious and the youth who stream to our Churches in Africa. She must work hard towards producing ethical and transformative servant leaders whose leadership will be a model and testimony of the decisiveness of good leadership for the future of the Church and society in Africa.

The fourth step is the need for a truly prophetic Church in Africa that is a poor Church for the poor in Africa. The future Church in Africa must always bear the marks and wounds of the suffering peoples of Africa in her proclamation, witnessing and ecclesial life. The two African synods spoke strongly of the need for the Churches of Africa to give hope to Africans by embracing an option for the poor (EA 139, 113, 70, 68–69, 44, 52; Africe Munus 25, 27, 29, 30, 84, 88–90). The greatest pastoral challenge facing the Churches in the complex social context of Africa today is how to proclaim and enact the praxis of hope to the poor in the cycle of inexcusable poverty which batter God's people in Africa. How can the presence of the Church in Africa become a point of light to bring about social transformation and abundant life in Africa? How can the Churches of Africa stand up against the dictatorship in some African countries, failed governments and institutions and the exploitation of the poor masses of our people? How do the Churches of Africa account for the rich human and material resources of the continent which are being exploited by African elites, religious and political leaders who are sometimes complicit in the international structures of exploitation which have kept Africa in thralldom for many centuries?

The Church of the future in Africa must speak through her words, ecclesial life, preaching and witnessing from within the chaos of the lives of many Africans who are still nailed to the cross. It must be a Church of accompaniment, an eye witness to what is happening to God's people and a travelling companion with the people of Africa, especially those on the margins. The decisiveness of this will be reflected in ecclesiologies which grow from the cries of the people and their living faith. It must give birth to new forms of liturgy, proclamation and witnessing which are translated into pastoral actions, performance and praxis of social transformation for human and cultural fulfilment as essential to integral salvation and the reversal of the unacceptable trajectory of history in Africa.

V A new communion between the Roman centre and the African margins

The fifth challenge is the emergence of true Catholicity in the spirit of the Second Vatican Council. Some of the questions which emerge in this regard are: Can the African Churches develop their own path to the future without being hampered by Roman supervision and control? When can the Church in Africa stand on her feet without her bishops and priests streaming to Europe and North America in search of financial help and of pastoral and administrative guidance from Rome? The Church of the future in Africa will need a new communion between the Roman centre and the Churches of Africa. This will require living fully the teaching of Vatican II on the ecclesial status of local Churches and local bishops. The Second Vatican Council's Dogmatic Constitution on the Church *Lumen Gentium* (23) teaches that there is an intimate, inseparable and mutual relation between the universal Church and the local Churches. The question then is how this plays out concretely in the relationship between Rome and the dioceses, national episcopal conferences, religious and lay Roman Catholic movements and institutes of consecrated life in Africa. Pope Francis's teaching is helpful here in understanding the right balance between Rome and the local Churches in this relationship.

Pope Francis uses the image of a great orchestra to describe the Catholicity of the Church: 'This is a beautiful image illustrating that the Church is like a great orchestra in which there is a great variety. We are not all the same, and we do not all have to be the same. We are all different, varied, each of us with our own special qualities. And this is the beauty of the Church: everyone brings their own gifts, which God has given, for the sake of enriching others. And between the various components there is diversity; however, it is a diversity that does not enter into conflict and opposition. It is a variety that allows the Holy Spirit to blend it into harmony.'[6] Francis also taught that the Church 'does not have simply one cultural expression' but rather it is in the diversity of peoples within the Church that we experience the gift of God and genuine catholicity (EG 115–116). He therefore calls for the acceptance in the Church of 'differing currents of thought in philosophy, theology, and pastoral practice' which are reconciled 'by the spirit of respect and love' and which help the Church grow in her understanding and application of the 'riches of God's Word.' (EG 41).

What Pope Francis teaches here is a guide on how the ecclesiology of Vatican II can be fully realized with regard to the status of local Churches. In an illuminative ecclesiology each local Church must be seen as a point of light which mirrors the common light which shines in the whole countenance of the Church through the Lord. This was already advocated in a different theological context before and immediately after Vatican II by future Pope Benedict XVI. Writing in the 1960s and 70s, Joseph Ratzinger challenged the 'universal claim of the Pope' and 'post-Constantinian patriarchal principle' which confused apostolic succession and primacy of the Pope with centralized administration 'tied up with political and geographical data.' He called for a clear distinction between episcopal theology in terms of the prerogatives of local bishops and papal theology in terms of apostolic succession, primacy and the handing on of the tradition. In this light, he argued that there can be 'a unity of faith and *communio*' between local Churches and the Pope wherein the Pope maintains the power to give 'binding interpretations of the revelation given in Christ whose authority is accepted whenever it is given.'[7]

Following from this insight, it is no longer necessary that the future Church should have a uniform liturgy, uniform canon law and the uniform appointment of local bishops by Rome, a uniform educational curriculum for all local Churches determined by the Congregation for the Evangelization of Peoples and a uniform pastoral plan and administrative structure. Indeed, I agree with Ratzinger that it is possible now to begin to think of the possibility of an African patriarchate. Such a patriarchate could cater to the ancient Coptic Churches of Africa, the Ethiopian Orthodox Churches and the Roman Catholic traditions in Africa, among others. The future Church of Africa should be untethered from its Roman yoke as a way of bringing to fullness truly African ecclesial traditions which can enrich the universal Catholic family only in the realized catholicity of the Church. Such an African patriarchate will be able to find contextual pastoral approaches and innovations to such questions as inculturated African liturgies, criteria for priestly and religious lives, marriage and family life, healing ministries in the Church, witchcraft and other unresolved pastoral challenges in Africa today, some of which are not even mentioned in the current *Catechism of the Catholic Church* and the *Code of Canon Law*.

69

VI Conclusion

A key ecclesiological principle for a vision of the future Church is one that Pope Francis gives in *Evangelii Gaudium* (222-225) which states that 'time is greater than space.' It is a principle which invites the Church to 'accept the tension between fullness and limitation.' Pope Francis invites the Church to be more concerned with 'giving priority to time', by patiently developing processes through openness to history, diversity, dialogue and synodality in the search for a missional praxis which can address the hunger of the world rather than trying to occupy or dominate spaces of power through self-assertion. This is an approach which can guide pastoral discernment, accompaniment and action in terms of being open to the surprises of the Holy Spirit (*Gaudete et Exsultate* [GE] 41) and long-term pastoral witnessing which builds up people and institutions. It requires fidelity to concrete human and cultural experiences in evangelization through 'attention to the bigger picture, openness to suitable processes, and concern for the long run' (EG 225).

The implication of time being greater than space is that the Church of the future should be open to embracing local processes in this era of World Christianity as a way of embracing the effulgence of the fruits of the Holy Spirit and the surprises of God. This challenges the Churches of Africa to embark vigorously and courageously on the path of reform. In order for this to happen, there is the need for greater space and freedom for local Churches in the Roman Catholic tradition. I am convinced that now is the time to release the primary energies of African Christians and Churches so that they can confront the peculiar challenges and limitations facing Africa, using her own spiritual and cultural resources in communion and co-responsibility with the Church of Rome. The Churches of Africa must not become slaves to the past or victims of an idealized future. The Church of the future in Africa can best serve the universal Church by being a servant of God's people in Africa and by being an agent in the liberation of our people from all that prevent them from enjoying the abundant life which emerges when God's will is done on earth as it is in heaven.

Notes

1. See S. Chu Ilo, *A Poor and Merciful Church: The Illuminative Ecclesiology of Pope Francis*, Maryknoll: Orbis Books, 2018.
2. Pope Francis's address to the bishops of Cameroon on their Ad Limina Visit, 6 September 2014, https://w2.vatican.va/content/francesco/en/speeches/2014/september/documents/papa-francesco_20140906_ad-limina-camerun.html.
3. See C. M. Galli, 'The Missionary Reform of the Church According to Francis: The Ecclesiology of the Evangelizing People of God', in A. Spadaro and C. M. Galli (eds.), *For a Missionary Reform of the Church: The Civiltà Cattolica Seminar*, New York: Paulist Press, 2017, pp. 24–30.
4. Ilo, *A Poor and Merciful Church*, p. 90.
5. See, Laurenti Magesa. *Anatomy of Inculturation: Transforming the Church in Africa.* Maryknoll, NY: Orbis Books, 2004, 148-155; Paulinus Odozor, *Morality Truly Christian, Truly Africa.* Notre Dame, Indiana: University of Notre Dame Press, 2014, 165-175.
6. Francis, *The Church of Mercy: A Vision for the Church.* Chicago: Loyola Press, 2014, 34.
7. K. Rahner and J. Ratzinger, *The Episcopate and the Primary*, vol. 4, New York: Herder and Herder, 1963, 57–59; J. Ratzinger, *Le nouveau peuple de Dieu*, Paris: Aubier, 1971, 68–70.
8. See the 1974 'Declaration of Bishops of Africa and Madagascar on the Promotion of Evangelization of Co-Responsibility and Promotion of Research on African Theology at the 4th Synod of World Bishops', in T. T. Tshibangu, *Le Concile Vatican II et L'Eglise Africaine: Mise en Oeuvre du Concile dans L'Eglise d'Afrique* (1960–2010), Paris: Epiphanie-Karthala, 2012, 129–132.

Part Three: Imagining the Church of the Future

Imagination and Fantasy: the Contribution of the Bible to the Church of the Future

MIKE VAN TREEK NILSSON

This essay draws from Scripture a necessary and radical reform in the Church (particularly in terms of biblical work). The Word is 'useful for life' since it nourishes symbolic imagination. Often sacred texts are read with a fundamentalist approach, and there is a lack of literary criteria and humanistic concern. Literature in today's world has diverse understandings of reality, and biblical work also highlights plurality. What is important is an emancipatory and plural understanding of reality. Due to encounters with the 'other', such understanding leads to an experience of God that is not self-centred. This essay offers criteria for changes in church and in society, and for including the Bible in humanistic studies.

The church of the future. It takes imagination and a sense of the fantastic to think about it. Gianni Rodari was a defender of the power of words; he both encouraged and trusted in the creativity of the child, who through play can conjure up a different world, connecting elements that ordinarily a logical, adult mind would want to keep separate. To take the floor in the field of theology trusting in the effectiveness of imagination and fantasy is no less than to challenge the possibilities of the present, such that within the church 'nobody might be enslaved'[1] but be free. Of course, imagination and fantasy on their own are not enough to reform the church; we would then need to debate, reflect, decide and lead change creatively through those ecclesiastical areas where there is a present lack of any evangelical path.

As of now, directing theological endeavour towards this approach seems to me to be a task that, without detracting from the discipline of its ways of working, actually goes beyond them, questioning as it does traditional assumptions as well as the usual theological methods. In fact, putting imagination as the driver of thought raises doubts about the institutional conditions of theological activity as much as about many of the centres where much of the systematic theological thinking has traditionally taken place. Centres that today no longer seem ready to embrace a new and audacious adventure but rather are more entrenched in a defence of their institutional approaches.

That theology might take on the challenges of the present day is a serious political question. The situations today's societies face as a consequence of globalization, demographic change, climate and migration, amongst others, also impact on the structure of the church. They call for innovative and creative responses. It is about how to help address the life challenges of life as we find them, for example, in the environmental crisis caused by an economic and political system that preys upon the earth and upon the dignity that has been ideologically nurtured by Christian tradition itself.

In addition to the socio-environmental crisis, many churches find themselves challenged for what is seen as inadequate responses to the culture of abuse of power that has developed as a basis of relationships both within society at large and internally. The lack of credibility and trust that this abuse of power has generated is increasingly notorious and apparent: the faithful, coming together not only amongst themselves but, quite rightly, with many other groups who do not share their faith, are making it clear that they do not trust their own pastors and guides.

The three elements that have been rapidly sketched, (socio-environmental crisis, abuse of power, and lack of credibility and trust in leaders) are signs of the complexity of the situation with which churches are living. A diagnosis of the crisis and the contextual characterisation, can lead to other perspectives. I would like to set out three of these. Each one requires a great deal imagination to be brought to bear when considering them. If we do not do this, we are destined to irrelevance and a repetition of approaches that are past their sell-by-date. What future can we envisage for the church and society if perspectives such as these are not challenged with radical imagination and fantasy?

In the forthcoming pages I am not going to seek to provide answers to this question, but rather to invite my readers to consider various aspects of biblical interpretation. Through my work as investigator and teacher and personal experience of reading the Bible, I have seen that certain elements of the way in which the Bible is read can shut down the freedom to be imaginative. This not only impoverishes the reading of a literary work but also makes routine an interaction with a text that should enthuse those who read it to encounter God. I shall deal successively with three aspects that seem important concerning the present ways in which the Bible is read: its positioning within a wide body of literature, the impact of politics and the role that the emancipation of the reader can play.

I The Bible as part of the universal literary constellation

Throughout history, the ways in which Christian churches and the faithful have related to Scripture have constantly changed. This is a pretty conclusive result of a consideration of the history of exegisis and approaches to reading the Bible in, for example the Reformation and Counter Reformation. Bible reading today is carried out by a myriad of interests, methods and perspectives. A democratization of the reader communities has taken place: the habitual reader is no longer, as five centuries ago, the Catholic clergy (exclusively white, educated European men). Today, contemporary themes and areas of interest have led, for example to readers who are, feminists, women , indigenous, liberationists etc.

All this does not mean that the Bible is abnormal. Individual and communal ways of reading Scripture are inscribed within the constellation of the customs and practice of reading of other texts. The Bible, in as much as it is a work that both enriches and is part of the great canon of universal literature, is read to help guide lives, to nourish the symbolic imagination that both explains and reads the work. It is a work that is both received critically by more or less erudite academics and by groups of lay initiates who correlate their own commentaries within the context of their own life experiences, understandings and knowledge of the world and all that lives within it.

It has always been said of the Bible that it can provide a word of truth or authority about the meaning of personal experience and how communities evolve. The attributive power to regulate community life and to direct thought lies at the heart of the canonicity of Scripture: it seeks to build a faithful community. But this characteristic is not exclusive to the Bible nor to the sacred texts. All literary work has some measure of impact on the readers and shapes them to an extent, bringing them together as an ideal community around the work. On another point, neither the Bible nor other literary works were written in isolation from society or culture. All such works from part of the flow of experiences, ideas, questions, intuitions, images, dreams and proposals that, in reality, are not the property of the author who writes them down, rather that he or she textualises them, placing them, in the case of narrative works, within a time frame that allows them to be received and elaborated upon by the readers. I therefore consider that the future of a nourishing reading of the Bible has to take on board this beautiful fact: that literature is something useful for life, it helps us to think about the possibilities of existence, to imagine, thanks to fiction, for example, new ways of living or to explore safely undesirable consequences of our actions.[2]

Thanks to the knowledge that we possess about the genesis and development of the various Bible writings, we understand that their compositional process did not differ from that of other contemporaneous documents. Because of this it is not unusual that the hermeneutics developed around Scripture do not differ either from those of other considered texts, sacred or not. On this point, although we cannot go into it here, it is important to bear in mind that the characteristic inspired by biblical texts, one which communities recognise in Scripture, as set out for example in 2 Timothy 3,16, is a proposition within the lines of argument developed by this epistle in the conflict provoked by several masters in their teachings aimed at women. It is regrettable that the way in which biblical inspiration is presented in many theological textbooks has insisted on the differences between the Greek and biblical conception of inspiration, signalling the distinctive characteristics of ecstatic possession in the Greek conception and in the latter, the Bible as the source of the revelation of God . This distinction has overvalued the informative content of the Bible, with its assertions and intellectual judgments, and has thus placed inspiration within a context of truth and an absence of faults.

However, a serious approach to study means we have to refine this distinction, since inspiration as ecstatic possession in which the poet connects with the divine, abandoning reason and literary skills, corresponds more or less to the conception of artistic inspiration developed by Plato. For her part, Penelope Murray concludes that the Greek concept of inspiration is more complex and rich than that sustained within Platonism. In Greece, the poet's knowledge is associated with memory, the execution of the poetic act and with the skills of the author. So she places more emphasis on the aspects of the literary art and culture of the author, him or herself.[3]

Paradoxically, biblical fundamentalism and most apologetic and integrationist Christian traditions, on the pretext of defending a distinct Christian identity, have always insisted on verbal inspiration. This seems much more akin to the platonic approach to inspiration than to what might be said about it based on the very scarce biblical or patristic references. In his address, the author of the second letter to Timothy expresses the usefulness of inspirational Scripture in taking forward a pedagogical approach to living in Christian piety. Scripture is useful because its strength is the Spirit of God. But that does not mean that its concept of inspiration implies the cancelling of all knowledge, experience and skill of the authors. Here, there is no major difference with the Greek conception as set out by Murray. The paradox in all of this is that one ends up considering as distinctive in Scripture, something from which, at the outset, Christianity wished to differentiate itself from. This arises from two fallacious approaches: first, the generalization of the platonic conception as being applicable to all of Greece and second, inadvertently applying the same characteristics that we have rejected, to biblical inspiration. Effectively, recovering the personality and writing skills of the authors of the Bible has been one of the most critical controversies in Catholic exegesis in the last century.

The challenge here would be to revisit and revise the theology of inspiration such that the literary character of Scripture can be more clearly perceived, that is to say, to stop considering the Bible as an exceptional and unique instance of literary production and be able to appreciate its singularity in the context of its forming part of a broader range of discursive outputs.

II Fundamentalism and hermeneutics special to the Bible

This approach that I am briefly setting out, taking into consideration a fundamental aspect of biblical hermeneutics such as is its divine inspiration, very intimately affects the treatment of Scripture in fundamentalist and traditional protestant and catholic circles. The rhetoric of these circles tends to identify the truth of Scripture through the assertive statements it contains. We have recently seen, for example in the restorationist proposals of various politicians, the strengthening of theses using arguments taken from Scripture.[4] Mary Ann Tolbert has shown the relationship between the political orientation of speeches and the kind of biblical hermeneutics used to develop arguments based on Scripture. Thus, political tendencies resistant to paths to emancipation (abolition, feminism, sexual 'minorities') make their arguments using 'special' biblical hermeneutics. That is to say, considering Scripture as a text for every particular, whose authority is established through its divine origin. So they emphasise the authority of the text – as well as their own role as its authentic interpreters – as being above any argument considered merely human. However, Tolbert also explains that Scripture has been an incentive or driver for many resistance struggles.[5] In Catholic circles, an acrimonious debate has recently started around what the traditional elements call, 'gender ideology'. The bone of contention for these groups is an artificial synthesis of biblical anthropology presented as a revelatory and unquestionable fact that can be imposed as a standard of judgement for anything else that is known about mankind. The writings of Paul Mankowski illustrate this.[6] He refers to the expression in Genesis 2,24, 'Therefore, a man shall leave his father and his mother and be joined to his wife, and they shall become one flesh' (according to his translation and from which I differ). For the Jesuit Mankowski, the verses affirm a 'transhistorical certitude' presented by the text as, 'detached from local, historical or even religious specificity'. The special hermeneutics of Scripture, that is to say the conception of what these signify, set the Bible apart from other literary works. This approach has been used to exclude and repress certain groups of churches by the disparagement of their requests or grievances. Considering this, Tolbert analyses cases of anti-racist struggles, feminism and claims for sexual diversity. The church of the future, on the other hand, is built on a principle of an absence of discrimination other than in the paradigm of a meeting. The church must show that the Word of God found in Sacred Scripture speaks to the full range of human experience: that it is textualised in Scripture and can enrich the reader's reflection without excluding perspectives that other cultures and traditions might have, expressed in their own literary texts, be they considered as sacred or not.

On this point, it seems to me that the future of faith communities lies through coming to value the plurality of perspectives to be found in Sacred Scripture. This plurality should not be accepted only as something that allows many men and women to find themselves either individually or in groups in the textual context, but rather as a challenge, a question that moves the focus placed on Christian identity towards a somewhat wiser reading of reality. Here I am interested in strengthening the idea that the books of Scripture have come about as part of a dialogue – and on many occasions as part of a dispute – with the currents of contemporary and subsequent cultures and politics. Faced with these cultural dynamics these books and biblical writings have attempted to advance a reflection in the minds of their readers and, though this, have an impact on their lives and the ordering of society.[7] Through this it can be seen that a political interpretation of Scripture is not an alternative to a theological one: the Bible, as a work of literature, works inside the reader helping him/her to understand, interpret and to change their own world.

III The emancipation of the reader

Access to reading has increased over the last hundred years. Sources of information on any and everything are ever closer and more accessible. The Bible has led the revolution in reading ever since the invention of printing, since it allowed, in the Europe of the Reformation, a multiplicity of theological debates which were able to circulate freely in spite of the strict control the roman Church imposed on the authors, printers, booksellers, book distributors etc.[8] Today, thanks to hypertext, access and navigation takes place amongst enormous quantities of information enabling is to talk of a time when the development of reading skills (selection, evaluation, registration, recovery of read texts for example) has acquired an importance not see hitherto. It is a matter, therefore, of educating emancipated readers, that is to say readers who are finding their pathway of liberation through Scripture, readers who can learn about life for themselves.

The emancipated reader is one who is not subject to an understanding of the Bible through the explanations (be they what they are) of teachers of grammar, or doctrine, since, as Rancière says, 'there is a dumbing down where one intelligence is subject to another.'[9] On the contrary, emancipation happens when the reader's knowledge is not subordinated to that of the teacher, when the reader's intelligence is not subjected to that of the teacher who explains. What I say may seem excessively distant from what we generally hear in academia: that the Bible is too complex for it to be understood without commentary, but this is not the point.

It is not a case of putting forward a self sufficient reading of the Bible, its is question of understanding that the Bible talks of the experiencing of God from a standpoint that is as much conditioned by culture as by our own experiences of God. So, reading Scripture, in reality, is to find oneself in conversation with another, someone who is not more right than me, but who offers a world that enriches the understanding and actions of the reader which are put into play within the world of the text and, in so doing, within their own world. Ricoeur called this '*Triple mimesis*'.[10] Just to express a note of caution about what has been said, it should be said that the Bible is not the only book that the faithful will read. At one time the Bible was the fundamental source of nourishment of western fantasy. Today's increasingly intense cultural interconnectivity brings together multiple accounts to feed the imagination.

The risk of an obsession with identity in churches is occurring once again: they want to immerse readers in a truth, a doctrine, a theology, a moral code, a code of obedience, a rite. This needs to be resisted; to fight against a uniformity of interpretation that stifles the dynamic of living beings. I believe that in so doing we can create a connection between the experiences of different peoples and cultures, making of this plurality something of value which leads to a coming together of the various groups and communities of readers and not to a merely tolerated side-by-side existence. Bible studies, the consideration and reading of the Bible, can play an important role in shaping democratic society. In order to do this, thought needs to be given to theology, and with it to the Bible within a context of the humanities. It was Martha Nussbaum who lucidly said that in order for the people of the world to be connected with their surroundings, they needed a 'narrative imagination' a 'capacity to think how it would be to be in the place of another, to interpret intelligently this other person's story and to understand the feelings, desires and hopes that they might have'.[11] I consider this to be the way forward: to develop strategies for reading that seek to understand the experiences textualised in the sacred books, to attempt to understand how an experience that goes beyond language has been given linguistic expression. I believe that reading the Bible will be significant in the process of emancipation and liberation only if it is read alongside other sacred texts, alongside other readers, believers or not, overcoming the barriers that Francesco Remotti has called, 'identity obsession'.

It will then, of course, be said that the *truth* of the Bible is being diluted in a relative multiplicity, that the Bible is being opened up to a world of all kinds of arbitrary interpretational approaches. That anything goes. That everything is certain because it is *my* truth. But it is not this at all! It is not a case of putting forward an individual(istic) interpretation, tailored to that I want to hear. It is about the existence of conversational spaces, of understanding the reading of Scripture as a meeting place for humanity and others' experiences of God. Of course, this calls for wise discernment, critical thinking and imagination. Discipline, work, intellectual honesty and freedom are the delights of the reader. The wise man Qoholet knew well of this when he said:

And I gave my heart to seek and search out by wisdom concerning all things that are done under heaven: this sore travail hath God given to the sons of man to be exercised therewith.
(Ecclesiastes 1,13).

Translated by Christopher Lawrence

Notes

1. G. Rodari. *Grammatica della fantasia. Inrduzione all'arte di inventare storie* (Trieste:El) 2010, p.10
2. On this topic: *T. Todorov. La Literatura en peligro* (Barcelona: Galaxia Gutenberg) 2009. In the field of theology A. Gesché has taken on board some of these ideas. In Latin America, see the work of Ivone Gebara, *Le mal au fémenin. Réflexions théologiques à partir du féminisme.* (Paris/Montréal: L'Harmattan) 1999. Regarding approaches to reading associated with this idea, I have found interesting teh porgramme fouded by Sarah Hirschman 'Gente y cuentos' (see http://peopleandstories.org).
3. P.Murray, 'Poetic Inspiration in Early Greece'. *The Journal of Hellenistic Studies* 101 (1981), p.100.
4. For example, the programmatic document of a government plan by Fabricio Alvarado, presidential candidate Costa Rica and who won the first round of elections, which places the Bible as one of the 'information sources' for the governments proposals of his 'party for national restoration' based on a 'Christian socialism' as an 'ideology for all'.
5. M.A.Tolbert, 'A New Teaching with Authority'. Segovia, Fernando – Tolbert, may Ann (eds.), *Teaching the Bible: The Discourses and Politics of Bible Pedagogy* (New York: Orbis Books) 1998.
6. P. Mankowski, 'La ensenza de Cristo sobre el divorcio y el segundo matrimonio: el dato Bíblico'. (tr. The teaching of Christ on divorce and second marriages: the Biblcial facts) Didaro, Robert (E.), *Permanecer en la verdad de Cristo: Matrimonio y communion en la Iglesia Católica.* (tr. *Keeping in the truth of Christ: Marriage and communion in the Church of Christ*). (Madrid:Cristiandad/Àgape) 2014, 38-68.
7. I have shown certain aspects of this dynamic in relation to the purity of the seed of Abraham in M. van Treek, 'Sara contra Esdras: Lectura crítica en el canon del Segindo Templo'. *Theología Xaveriana* 67 (2017), 163-185 [http://dx.doi.org/10.1114/javeriana. tx67-183.scelcc]. Amongst the texts in the canon can be found an actual dispute between various currents of thought that reinforce nationalist ideas of identity and texts that seek to defuse them.
8. On this see D.Julia, 'Lecturas y Contrareforma'. Cavallo, G.-R. Chartier, *Historia de la lectura en el mundo occidental* (Madrid: Santillana) 2004, 415-467.
9. J. Rancière. *El maestro ignorante: conco lecciones sobre la emancipación intellectual* (Santiago de Chile: Huerders/Libros del Zorzal) 2014, p. 27.
10. P.Ricoeur. *Tiempo y narración 1: Configuración del tiempo en el relato histórico* (México/Buenos Aires: Siglo XXI) 2004
11. M.Nussbaum. *Nor for profit: why democracy needs the humanities*, Princeton, N.J: Princeton University Press. Also see: *Sin fines de lucro: por qué la democracia necesita de las humanidades* (Buenos Aires: Katz) 2010, pág. 132.

What Structures are Needed for a Reform of the Church?

SERENA NOCETI

The effort to imagine a future Church must inevitably face the limitation of being within a particular historical period, marked by the reception of Vatican II, which is a process very far from being concluded. The Second Vatican Council made it clear cannot be simply thought of as the restoration of a model belonging to past history such as that defined by the Council of Trent, but has to be based on a global regeneration, both able to go beyond the Eurocentrism that has marked the recent centuries of its history, and by leaping the rigid barrier between clergy and laity and involving the whole people of God in this process of transformation. Pope Francis' Apostolic Exhortation Evangelii Gaudium *has provided important ideas to start us thinking and launch this transformation process. This means radically rethinking the role of the local churches and recognising the value of inherited culture and traditions for far too long sacrificed by a vision of centralised uniformity. It is also necessary to encourage structures of synodal procedure as normal to encourage the participation of all the baptised in the taking of decisions that govern the lives of Christian communities.*

As long ago as the first phase in the reception of Vatican II, Karl Rahner called for the whole Church to think about a 'structural transformation of the Church, as a task and an opportunity', in the words of an essay from 1972.[1] The three demands that structure the book – 'Where are we?', 'What do we have to do?' 'How can we imagine the Church of the future?' – are also a valuable guide for our thinking today. They send us back to Vatican II's vision of the Church as an essential standard and pointer to the future, while at the same time indicating the limitations of the documents and outlining the form that might be taken by a possible and necessary reception of the Council.

I In Transition: between 'no longer' and not yet

'We must grow up in every way into him who is the head, into Christ' (Eph 4.15)

Whatever act of 'theological and pastoral imagination' relating to the Catholic Church of the future forms part of the still open process of reception of the Council: we are saying goodbye to the Tridentine and post-Tridentine model of church organisation. This has accompanied Catholic experience for over five centuries and shaped ideas, spirituality and pastoral life, but we have to recognise that the transformation of the Church outlined by Vatican II has not yet fully arrived. The pontificate of Pope Francis, with his decisive adoption of the Council's pastoral approach and of the call for reform that motivated the calling of the Council and marked its progress (both in the Roncalli version of *aggiornamento* and the Montini version of 'renewal') undoubtedly represents a new phase in the reception of Vatican II, in a socio-cultural setting profoundly changed from that of the 1960s, for a Church that has now become worldwide, as predicted by Karl Rahner. The Apostolic Exhortation *Evangelii Gaudium*, which contained the programme for the pontificate, is basically a call to measure ourselves in a new way against the ecclesiological and ecclesial vision of Vatican II, by abandoning the Eurocentric outlook and drawing on the Church practices and theological proposals of theologians and bishops in different continental settings and in the face of new languages, challenges and issues.[2] The stated aim is the '(re)creation' – in the plurality of local churches – of the *forma ecclesiae*, on the basis of a dynamic of evangelisation that involves all the people of God in an hermeneutical process of the gospel in the history of our time. It is not a matter of deducing from the ecclesiological premises of the documents of Vatican II a complete Church model (one and only one) to be applied, but to (re) activate those communicative and participatory forces in which, by the power of the Spirit, the We of the Church can be regenerated through the interaction of the protagonists (laity and ordained ministers) who together make it up.

At the same time, it would be naïve to think that 'the aim of encouraging ongoing missionary renewal [among all members of the Church]' *(Laudato si'*, 3) could be achieved without a review – with a bold and sceptical eye – of the long period since the Council to identify the factors of resistance to reform and to the reforms initiated or hoped for by the Council. After all, it is impossible to underestimate the impact of an official hermeneutic, first, of the Council documents and then of the very process of the reception of Vatican II, which, in the name of consolidating and preserving true doctrine in the face of possible theological and ethical relativisms and reductionisms, in fact blocked promising theological investigations, ecumenical dialogues and changes in pastoral methods and in the end marginalised or abandoned key perspectives of Vatican II's vision of the Church (an ecclesiology based on the local church and no longer in a universalistic perspective, an ordained ministry based and defined in terms of ecclesiological function, the definition of the Church as the people of God, reading the signs of the times, etc.).[3]

The aim of this article is therefore not to assemble a series of elements that would form an ideal image of the Church, as many valuable theological studies have done since the 1990s,[4] but to discuss the conditions and premises of a reform that considers the Church subject in its institutional dynamic and its structures. The socio-cultural context of late modernity to which we belong requires us not only to abandon the traditional ecclesiological categories, which stressed a Church with an a-historical essence and be open to a vision of the people of God typified by its historical character, but also to review radically the way in which ecclesiological theories are constructed, in dialogue with social sciences and philosophies. It is not sufficient to develop new concepts or take on new discoveries, nor is it enough to assert in theory the protagonism of some actors, lay people or women, in order to change immediately Church institutions, the organisation, the life-form of the ecclesial body, pastoral practices: in this epochal transition what is at stake is a transformation of the collective body known as 'Church', which has dynamically to reshape every aspect of its form – guiding visions, languages, protagonists, internal and external relations, activities and procedures, a social system. It is this general process that is being promoted, accompanied, encouraged, because what we are facing here is an incremental change or an alteration that does not affect the collective culture of the social body, but a true Church reform that affects and reshapes everything.

II Reform: visions, relationships, structures
'building itself up' (Eph 4.16)

Students of the sociology of institutions and organisations and experts in political science remind us – on the basis of very diverse theories of social phenomena –[5] of the fact that every reform comes into effect simultaneously on three levels: on the contents of collective awareness, on the form of internal relationships, and on structures, procedures and roles through which the social body is expressed and maintained. Any reform that hopes to be successful must affect these levels simultaneously and in a coherent way, knowing that in every case an understanding in collective awareness is underpinned by a particular relational form and a given structure, but that these relationships and structures need to be supported by a 'shared vision' of the Church. It is not enough to educate individuals on the level of ideas: the relational form must be redesigned, and a change introduced in the way ecclesial relationships are institutionalised; at the same time in this process of transformation structures combine an objective and operational function with a symbolic and communicative dimension. To understand and institution and think about how to reform it involves asking oneself how people 'create' meanings through common experiences, through interpretations of stories, rituals, symbols, myths and through individual and collective practices, and implies questioning ourselves about how groups and individuals *acquire* and *reinterpret* such meanings on the basis of a socio-cultural setting of which they are part an which is in permanent evolution.[6] The process of reform is fed by the awareness that the form and structures in which ecclesial experience and action take place are not immutable and so always open to change, from the moment in which 'we no longer have in a chemically pure form the immutable central substance alongside a specific form, but we have the former only through the historical mediation of the moment'.[7]

So what is required is not simply a readjustment of the current Church structures (largely inherited from Trent), or to replace them one by one as part of reforms *in* the Church, but to initiate a general process

88

of reform of the Church itself operating on the three levels mentioned above. Linear models of intervention that concentrate on just one level or on a single change factor are not adequate: renewal of the institution has to be envisaged in a logic of complexity, starting from the dynamics of social construction of meaning (in an interaction of personal faith and Church tradition), from the interaction between the protagonists, through the interconnection of structure and social action.

Pope Francis has stressed the value of the process that unfolds in time (LG 223) and the need to rethink objectives structures, styles and methods (EG 33), has reminded us that reform of structures requires pastoral conversion and must generate new convictions and attitudes (EG 27, 189); he has warned against the security that can be derived by structures (EG 49). But how are we to move from the phase of symbolic deconstruction and reconstruction of the papacy and the way the Church is presented in public, with a determined appeal to Gospel principles, and from the call for a new form of Church (poor, merciful, inclusive, at the service of all, etc.) – that have marked these first five years of Francis' pontificate - to a reform that also affects the structures of the world's biggest institutions, with a history measured in centuries, which exists embodied in a multiplicity of cultural settings? How can a reform be promoted and controlled, not only on the level of paradigms but also on that of social structures?

III (Re)visions: (Incomplete) Prospects for a Church to be (Re) formed

'the whole body, joined and knitted together'

As is well known, the documents of the Second Vatican Council explicitly touch on the topic of Church reform in only a few passages, though these are significant: they justify it by the historical nature of the Church (LG 48) and the limitations and sin that call for renewal and purification (LG 8, 48), and set out the criteria for it (UR 4, 6). Some changes in structure were envisaged by the Council (or defined immediately after it ended), whether in the Constitution on the Sacred Liturgy or in the decrees dealing with the various groups of the faithful (priests, religious, laity, seminarians, missionaries). More than 50 years after the end of Vatican II, it is possible to attempt an evaluation of these, though the space available in this article means that they will be summarised and simplified. In the first place, we may note that significant results have been achieved through a liturgical reform that affected in various ways the shape of the Church, the languages, structures and the whole action of the liturgy. Secondly, the changes that took place in the life and ministry of bishops, priests, lay people and religious have been undoubtedly profound, but have not (yet) led to an overall redefinition of the Church body in its key dynamics; they have dealt with the individual protagonists and their role in the existing Church institution, but they have not adequately rethought the relational dynamics existing between these subjects, which determine Church identity. An important gap can been seen in the conciliar documents: there is no specification of structures and institutions that would have made it possible to bring to pass what is said in the 'constitutional charter' that constitutes Chapter 2 of *Lumen Gentium*, which defines the principles underlying membership of the Church, the shape of the people and the common messianic mission, the constitutive processes of the *communio* deriving from the proclamation of the Gospel, the relations between the protagonists and the inculturation of the faith. It is precisely this absence and the fact that the only structures it specified in any detail were those linked to the episcopate and primacy (such as the synod of bishops, bishops' conferences, the Roman curia and diocesan curias), that show that Vatican II did not completely abandon the Gregorian-Tridentine hierarchical model: there is no outline of a dynamic organisation, an 'institutional form', for a Church developed on the basis of the asserted dignity of the baptised, nothing that would ensure the real participation of all in 'being Church'. The Church was not envisaged as an open social system that evolves in history as a result of the (plural and diversified) word spoken by all the faithful. How can equality in baptismal dignity be affirmed if this is not respected in adequate institutional forms of co-responsibility and is not guaranteed or safeguarded in the institutions? How can the relation between the protagonism in the Church between the faithful, the ministerial nature of the Church, (ordained) ministers and the mission of the laity, presented in Chapters II-IV of *Lumen gentium* be made a reality without a structural reform of the Church that affects roles and functions, rights and duties and exercise of powers? In this Vatican II shows itself to be incomplete: it was unable to set out, alongside its renewed ecclesiological vision, a dynamic plan for reform and adequate institutions that would promote and energise it.

IV Transfiguration: *Traditio Ecclesiae* and Church Structures
'*by every ligament with which it is equipped*' (Eph 4.16)

The aim of the Gregorian and Tridentine reforms was *reformatio in capite et in membris*, 'reform in head and members', which gave priority to the twofold dynamic of communication and decision-making, 'top-down' and 'centre-periphery'.[8] The Tridentine decrees *de reformatione* concentrated basically on one element of the Church body (priests and bishops), endowed with appropriate powers (sacral and jurisdictional), and insisted, in a normative style, on their *mores* (in the sense of public action), on the exercise of their offices and on their formation (seminaries). In a 'homogeneous institution' like the Tridentine Church, in which uniformity is an essential value and the *unio* of believers and the achievement of the constitutive ends are guided by the principle of delegated authority, reform involved the obtaining of a complete 'theory' of the Church, entrusted to the 'superior and intermediate cadres', endowed with adequate recognised authority and of the promotion of social and organisational structures consistent with this vision (parish, catechism, missal, seminary, pastoral visitations).

Much more complex is the task of the reception of Vatican II, which, far from being a mere application of the letter of the documents, is a process of Church transformation, acceptance of the event and what is affirmed in the literary and doctrinal corpus formed by the conciliar texts. The ecclesiological renewal brought about by Vatican II in relation to the Tridentine vision is profound: the first principle that establishes the Church, generates and regenerates it, is in the proclamation of the gospel of the Kingdom. The Church lives 'in tradition', in a communication of the faith and in faith among believers, ordained ministers and laity, whose identity and dignity are radically reimagined (*Lumen gentium*, Chapters II-III): the local church is envisaged as the 'basic form' of this process of being Church. To promote Church reform according to Vatican II involves looking at structures not as static and standardised (as a sort of container of activities, designed to ensure stability), but as frames in and through which the social action (evangelisation, liturgy, witness) of individuals and the collective body 'Church' ensures the process of ecclesial life. The focus is not on 'fixed institutions', but on 'institutionalising forces'.

To be adequate to the Church of the future, culturally polycentric, with all protagonists actively participating, the Church structures (and the related social actions) will have to respond first to three instances necessary to a Church in tradition that wishes to face the challenges already present today: to preserve plurality, guarantee interconnection, and maintain identity during evolution. The necessary inculturation of the Christian faith in different languages and different social and organisational forms (which will probably require the drafting of Codes of Canon Law for each continent), must be related to structures that express and bring about the *una Catholica*. The contribution of the many protagonists who together make up the Church (individual believers, local churches) includes the development of structures for interaction, which will bring into being the pluri-directional dynamics of communication proposed in *Dei Verbum*, 8 and *Lumen gentium*, 12, by means of a real *consensus fidelium*. The tension created by definitions in stable and codified forms (which will finish by being sacralised and treated as immutable, become exempt from evolution and 'ossified') can be recognised as a logic inherent in any social body, but will also be counteracted by the establishment right from the beginning of elements and procedures of verification and rethinking, safety fuses and procedures for listening to those who do not belong or who express critical views of the status quo.

V Semper reformanda: dynamics and life forms of the people of God

'as each part is working properly, promotes the body's growth in building itself up' (Eph 4.16)

Very often in the course of the last five years, Pope Francis has stressed the maxim *Ecclesia semper reformanda*, and there is an obvious need for a process of transformation that resumes the interrupted process of the reforms advocated by Vatican II and affects some sectors of Church life that seem particularly fragile.[9] It seems essential to concentrate on the reforms of the dynamics that are at the heart of the life and evolution of the

Church as a body, because this will make it possible to identify processes that are irreversible and above all create conditions that will make it possible to face the challenges that the future will bring for believers, but which today we can at the most guess at.[10] More specifically, in the agenda of the reception of Vatican II, the central question is that of the dynamics, the institutions and the structures that will make it possible to create the sort of people described in Chapter II of *Lumen gentium*. Thinking and action for reform must therefore move along three vectors, around which a real change in the form of Church relationships: change the models of communication, rethink power(s) and authority, and recognise 'forgotten partners', lay men and lay women. All three are involved in recent socio-cultural metamorphoses. All three have to do with the mediations that structure any social body, and which need to be reviewed and reshaped in the reforms; in the interaction of the three it is possible to remodel in a new way the dialectical relationship between the 'objective structure of relationships' in the Church and the 'subjective efforts at constructing' collective meaning (P. Bourdieu).

5.1 Questions of communication: The Church is born and lives through communicative interactions

The Church is an institutionalised collective subject, socially constructed through communicative interactions, in evolution: all participatory dynamics, symbolic and liturgical, in decision-making or operations, can be traced back to such communicative interactions, with declaratory and performative aims.[11] Behind every model of Church there is always a specific communicative model that supports, upholds and keeps in being the ecclesial subject, whether through dynamics of transmission of or witness to the faith for those who are not believers or through dynamics of witness and interpretation of faith and in the faith among those who already belong to the ecclesial body. Reform of the Church requires first promotion and structuring of pluri-directional and asymmetrical communicative dynamics (allowing for the differences that exist on the charismatic and ministerial level among the faithful) that will make it possible to leave behind the Gregorian and Tridentine model of Church, with its one-directional communications system. Every person is a transmitter-receiver in the 'dialogue network' of the Church and involved in the communication of the faith that brings the Church into being because he or she is invested with the prophetic office (LG 12): the authority of the ordained ministers does not impose the desired change, but promotes the process of community discernment that leads towards the *consensus fidelium*, and is the guarantor of ecclesial identity in the Tradition, as custodian of the apostolic character of the proclamation, which can, finally and as a result of the hermeneutical process involving all the components of the Church, pronounce publicly and in the liturgy the word of the church which is us. A Church that wants to make a reality of its synodal nature has to reconfigure itself on its various levels (from parishes to dioceses and the universal Church) to form 'hermeneutical communities' with spaces and structures for listening and participation, and acquire a style of communication sensitive to polyphony that will make it possible to receive new perspectives, new languages, new categories that have been opened up and entrusted to those Church subjects (lay people, women, young people, people who belong to non-Western cultures) who until today have not received adequate recognition in the ecclesial body.

5.2 Questions of power: powers and exercise of authority in the ecclesial body

'Power is the most important aspect of a society's structure.'[12] The acquisition of authority roles, the distribution of power or powers and their organisation into a hierarchy, the basis and justification of power and its associated roles, play a central part in any social system. For centuries Catholicism has institutionalised a 'simple', pyramidal form of authority, starting from the 'one', with some involvement of 'some' and directed at the 'all', who were required to give obedience, justified by a set of ideas and values, some explicit and some implicit, of a religious nature.[13] In this model social power, which controls the attribution of statuses to the various subjects (defining the role and position of each), and cultural power, linked to the creation, interpretation and maintenance of values and meanings, have been appropriated and embodied by the same subjects, the priest and the bishop. But the social and cultural change that has taken place in the West in the last three centuries has been far-reaching and has inevitable repercussions on the experience of the Church: crises of traditional (kyriocentric and patriarchal) authority, the development of a democratic mindset, obsessive anti-authoritarianism and recognition of the value of individual self-determination, multiplication of centres of power, abandonment of any directly religious legitimation of authority.

The Gregorian and Tridentine ecclesiological model of the Church as *societas* developed around the principle of delegated authority, with an understanding of power in the logic of one-person rule – pope, bishop, priest – over the 'all', whose role was assent and obedience. Vatican II, with its shift of focus from the two *potestates* to the *tria munera Christi* that define the common messianic mission and are then instantiated in specific forms by the different subjects (ordained ministers and lay people), offers the prospect of a general rethinking of the basis and nature of power: we have to develop a plural vision of 'powers', with a view to a responsibility of Us, the Church, that is always shared, to distributing the *exousia*, the 'power to', the word that brings the Church into being that is entrusted to the disciples of Jesus, in order then to rethink according to this logic any 'power over', especially that of the ordained ministers in the community, and to face the thorny question of gender for those for whom the power of the 'one' in the Catholic Church is always defined as male; we have to recognise forms of *potestas iurisdictionis* deriving from baptism. A Church reform today demands the presence of a 'transformative leadership', exercised in collegial form: a person who has authority in the Church has to combine analysis and imagination, must be able to steer general processes of change by integrating, encouraging internal dialectic, stimulating different paths towards the common goal. Pastoral teams, formed by ordained ministers, married people, lay people, men and women, are the primary structures to develop an ecclesial body that gives primacy to the logic of shared power as a medium and expression of a synodal mode of relationship, escaping from the fascination of the power of the 'one', which is always exposed to the danger of self-referentiality. In every case the longed- for involvement of the laity in pastoral decisions demands a more complex process of decision-making, divided into more stages so that the competences and experience of the laity influence the issues to be discussed right from the start, so that there is the possibility to express reasoned and shared proposals (that may involve a vote) with a view to the final decision by the ordained minister, which could not imaginably ignore the overall process carried out by the community, since *quod omnes tanget ab omnibus tractari [et aprobari] debet* ('What affects all should be discussed [and decided] by all').[14]

5.3 Questions of recognition: forgotten subjects, roles, interactions

In the end any process of reform develops around the maturation of awareness and the roles of the various actors involved. J.J. O'Malley reminds us that the Tridentine model started with the reorganisation and revitalisation of the diocesan clergy, placing at the centre the idea of the parish, from where the cure of souls was ensured. In the case of Vatican II, the primary agents of bringing the Church into being and making the reform effective are all the faithful, whether ordained ministers or laity: the identities and protagonism of each are defined in common relation to the one mission and to the internal dynamics of communication and participation. Pope Francis goes beyond the reductive and ultimately regressive hermeneutics of recent decades, highlights the dignity of the laity, who 'are, put simply, the vast majority of the people of God' (EG 102), especially women (EG 103-104), all sharing responsibility and not mere collaborators of the hierarchy (as the 1997 *Instruction Ecclesia de mysterio* insisted), but with their own word that is necessary for a renewed understanding of the Gospel at out moment in history. For centuries relationships within the Church have been focused on the undisputed centrality of the clergy, with the role of the laity undervalued and even belittled; even today the ordained ministers determine the language of the institutional Church, the boundaries of membership, public activities; investment goes almost exclusively to the training of clergy and even the suggestions for the reorganisation of the parish system in Europe are related exclusively to the presence and action of priests. There can be no doubt that the problem is one of empowering the laity, especially women, but their power of agency depends – at a deeper level – on a question of entitlement; creating the conditions for them to make a contribution does not depend only on their attitude, but on the expectations of the social body, on the forms of interaction that have been established and on who enjoys authority over the rest of us and can recognise or not the right and duty to participate. The process of reforming Church structures must therefore operate on more levels, in a way that involves at the same time and in combination the training and agency of all the actors who together make up the Church. We have to promote structures of ordinary synodal practice (consultations, assemblies on specific topics, production of collective documents, local synods to prepare for synods of bishops, etc.), which allow for a wider participation of all the baptised, with no restrictions to representatives or delegates of councils, consultations of the laity; we need to increase the spaces for discussion, decision-making and training in which the competent and authoritative voice of women can be heard;[15] we have to rethink the authority of ordained ministers, at long last accepting the new theological ideas of Vatican II and picking up the issues left on one side (the choice of presbyters from celibates and married men, the ordination of women deacons, training courses for bishops, promotion of the permanent male diaconate, the abolition of seminaries and a rethinking of the process of training priests, and the role of the diocesan clergy as a group). Real choices in this area can no longer be postponed, as Edward Schillebeeckx was arguing as long ago as the 1980s: an enormous number of Christian communities, in some countries as many as 70%, cannot celebrate the Sunday Eucharist for want of priests. The awareness of the centrality of the Eucharist for Christian life is pressing us to reopen the discussion of the criteria for admission to the ministry and of the traditional forms in which it is exercised.

VI Conclusion

Action to transform the models of communication within the Church, the 'architecture' of power relations, starting with the power of utterance that brings the Church into being, and the dynamics of the recognition of dignity, makes it possible to have a profound impact on the Church's vital process, without wasting energy on sectoral reforms, probably less complex and with the likelihood of more rapid results, and without designing proposals that are too detailed, which would risk becoming outdated given the speed of cultural changes. Some of the steps suggested here as regards the reconfiguration of Church roles and functions, and the definition of powers and the exercise of authority, obviously involve a confrontation with the magisterium at the level of the universal Church, but other transformations, relating to models of communication and organisation, can already be proposed and put into operation at the level of local and particular churches, allowing for the cultural sensitivities in

Serena Noceti

play, for example in practices and models involving gender. Prophetic experiments, promoted by bishops conferences or regional bodies, or developed in diocesan context, including those initiated or suggested by the laity, could support and guide future debates and studies on a larger scale. As Ulrich Beck wrote in his incomplete posthumous work, 'It is necessary to explore the new beginnings, to focus on what is emerging from the old and seek to grasp future structures and norms in the tumult of the present.'[16]

Translated by Francis McDonagh

Notes

1. K. Rahner, *The Shape of the Church to Come*, London 1974.
2. Among the many studies published on this topic, cf. J.I. Segovia et al., *Evangelii gaudium y los desafíos pastorales para la Iglesia*, Madrid 2014; K. Appel – J.H. Deibl (ed.), *Barmherzigkeit und zärtliche Liebe. Das theologische Programm von Papst Franziskus*, Freiburg i Br. 2016; G. Mannion (ed.), *Pope Francis and the Future of Catholicism*, Cambridge 2017.
3. Cf. A. Melloni – G. Ruggieri (ed.), *Chi ha paura del Vaticano II?*, Rome 2009; G. Routhier, *Il Concilio Vaticano II. Recezione ed ermeneutica*, Milano 2007; A. Melloni – C. Theobald (ed.), Vatican II: a Forgotten Future, *Concilium* 4/2005; M. Faggioli, *Vatican II. The Battle for Meaning*, New York 2012; M. Faggioli – A. Vicini (ed.), *The Legacy of Vatican II*, Mahwah, NJ, 2015.
4. Cf G. Lafont, *Imagining the Catholic Church*, Collegeville MN, 2000; M. Kehl, *Wohin geht die Kirche?*, Freiburg im Br., 1996; J.B. Libanio, *Cenários da Igreja*, São Paulo, 1999; C. Duquoc, *Je crois en l'Église*, Paris 1999; G. Lafont, *L'Église en travail de réforme*, Paris, 2011; S. Dianich, *La chiesa cattolica verso la sua riforma*, Brescia 2014.
5. Cf N. Brunsson, *Reform and Routine. Organizational Change and Stability in the Modern World*, Oxford 2009; M. Ferrante – S. Zan, *Il fenomeno organizzativo*, Rome 200711, pp 214-250; J.G. March – J.P. Olsen, *Rediscovering Institution. The Organizational Basis of Politics*, New York 1989; J.G. March, *Explorations in Organizations*, Stanford 2008, pp 191-296; D.C. North, *Institutions, Institutional Change and Economic Performance*, Cambridge, 1990; G.R. Bushe – R.J. Marshak (ed.), *Dialogic Organization Development*, Oakland CA 2015.
6. Cf. P.L. Berger – T. Luckmann, *The Social Construction of Reality*, New York, 1966.
7. W. Kasper,' Zum Problem der Rechtgläubigkeit in der Kirche von morgen', in *Various, Lehre der Kirche – Skepsis der Gläubigen*, Freiburg i.Br. 1970, p. 79, quotation from F.X. Kaufmann, *Sociologia e teologia*, Brescia 1974, p. 179.
8. Cf J. O'Malley, *Developments, Reforms, and Two Great Reformations, in Tradition and Transition: Historical Perspective on Vatican II*, Wilmington, DE, 1989, pp 82-125.
9. Cf the suggestions in A. Spadaro - C.M. Galli (ed.), *La riforma e le riforme nella chiesa*,

Brescia 2016.
10. Cf. N. Ormerod, *Re-visioning the Church. An Experiment in Systematic-Historical Ecclesiology*, Minneapolis 2014; L.S. Mudge, *Rethinking Beloved Community*, Washington 2001; R. R. Gaillardetz – E.D. Hahnenberg (ed.), *A Church with Open Doors. Catholic Ecclesiology for the Third Millennium*, Collegeville MN, 2015.
11. S. Noceti, 'Eucaristia e soggetto del pensare cristiano', in F. Scanziani (ed.), *Eucaristia e Logos. Un legame propizio per la teologia e la chiesa*, Milan, 2013, pp 183-212.
12. B. Jessop, *Social Order, Reform and Revolution. A Power, Exchange, and Institutionalization Perspective*, Herder & Herder Mew York 1972, 54. Cf. Cf. S.R. Clegg, *Frameworks of Power*, London 1989; S.R. Clegg – M. Haugaard (ed.), *Handbook of Power*, London 2009.
13. N. Timms – K. Wilson (ed.), *Governance and Authority in the Roman Catholic Church*, London 2000; P. Prodi – L. Sartori (ed.), *Cristianesimo e potere*, Bologna 1986; T.P. Rausch, *Authority and Leadership in the Church. Past directions and Future*, Wilmington DE, 1989; G. Mannion, 'What do we Mean by "Authority"?', in B. Hoose (ed.), *Authority in the Roman Catholic Church. Theory and Practice*, Aldershot 2002, pp 19-36; G. Mannion – R. Gaillardetz – J. Kerkohs – K. Wilson, *Readings in Church Authority*, Aldershot 2003; M.N. Ebertz, *Dienstamt, Macht, Herrschaft in Kirche und Gesellschaft*, in M. Remenyi (ed.), *Amt und Autorität*, Paderborn 2012, pp 115-138.
14. Y.M. Congar, in *Revue historique de droit français et étranger* 36 (1958), 210-259.
15. Cf. C. Militello – S. Noceti (ed.), *Le donne e la riforma della chiesa*, Bologna, 2017.
16. Ulrich Beck, *The Metamorphosis of the World*. Cambridge and Malden MA, 2016: ebook, p. 27.

The Community of the Church: Walking in Step with the Spirit in Digital Culture

This essay explores digital culture and advocates for how the Church can be a pro-active presence in this context especially if attentive to three critical socio-cultural developments wrought by digital communication technologies: truthfulness, potential for authentic encounters, and shifting notions of authority. By emphasizing the work of the Holy Spirit as both constitutive of Church but also transformative for each of these three developments, the essay proposes building on pneumatological foundations toward a future Church, one that can be a prophetic and pro-active witness in digital culture.

I Introduction

Considering the work of the Holy Spirit is integral to the task of this collection of essays on imagining a future Church. This essay reflects on the community of the Church as it might emerge in the future especially in light of the advent of digital culture as one socio-cultural reality shaping life in our world today. Imagining the community of the Church in the future is a task beholden to pneumatology – to the theology of the Holy Spirit, and more specifically what we know about the Spirit's work of animating the Church. Along these lines, this essay builds upon key pneumatological points, both essential to Church but also especially relevant to life in a digital age. Digital culture, as a culture defined by communication technologies also has the potential for deep resonance with pneumatology, as communication in the theological sense is a Spirit-

101

led activity. In imagining the community of the Church in the future, this essay therefore is built around the Holy Spirit, and specific characteristics of the work of Spirit that are especially salient for thinking about Church, communication and digital culture. These characteristics include truth, life and power. Taking these each in turn, this essay will discuss their resonance for digital culture and offers directions forward toward a future Church.

Our world is always changing. Yet, with the advent of digital communications technologies, our world has undoubtedly changed in a remarkable way. Within a relatively short span of time, our ability to access, share and contribute to the flow of information has greatly expanded. In 2018 most of us take mobile media and ease of access to social communication for granted, and the contemporary generation of lay and ordained ministers see digital communication as part of the everyday reality of serving people and sharing the Gospel. In discussing our world so shaped by digital communication technologies, we are properly speaking about a digital culture, rather than just a set of tools or electronic gadgets that we have. Our use of these tools and gadgets has been profoundly impactful on the way we live our lives, interact with one another and with the world and the way we seek out, obtain and contribute to the flow of information available to us. As a result, we are living, thinking, interacting differently today, whether we are 'online' or 'offline', which is a distinction that has become obsolete due to the ubiquity of the impact of communication technologies. We are always online, that is, thinking and behaving in a way that reveals the constant connectivity available to us.

This cultural shift has remarkable advantages but also poses some considerable challenges. The ease with which we are able to access and share information and to connect with people instantly is truly a great benefit. At the same time, navigating the constant availability of information and connection has some pitfalls. In 2018 we are struggling with authenticity and truthfulness of information and being able to distinguish truth from fake news. We are navigating how to still forge respectful, mutual human encounters with one another when these are mediated by words and images that appear on a screen. We are also grappling with the notion of authority: who selects the information we are able to see and receive, who has a voice to contribute to the greater cultural narratives being told, who has the influence to 'trend' or be heard. In the midst of this, the Church has a blessed opportunity to communicate the Good News to speak especially to these and other areas of contention in our world. As discussed below, each of these areas of truth, civil conversation and authority resonate with characteristics of the Spirit of truth, life and power.

Often, our pastoral planning conversations around digital culture take on a tone of urgency about keeping up with the times, keeping up with what 'young people' are doing, all from the place of reacting to the shifts wrought by digital culture. This essay proposes another approach, which is for the Church to take a pro-active stance toward this cultural reality, and to recall our original mandate of communicating the Gospel to all the world.[1] We are called to be communicators of the Gospel regardless of the technologies available to us, and this call precedes digital or other revolutions in social communication. One hope of this essay is for the future Church to be a pro-active community that proclaims the Gospel in ways that not only speak to but also shape life in the digital age, guiding society toward authenticity, truth and encounter. We can do this by attentively listening and reading the signs of the times, paying close attention to the challenges and tensions that arise in our world today and proclaiming the possibility of life lived abundantly in the midst of these.

For the Church then, this remarkable cultural shift introduces the opportunity and the challenge of presenting the Gospel in new ways, in new contexts and speaking to new needs and suffering. Given that the Word of God and the Spirit of God both imbue the communication of the Gospel, the Church's task in the digital age is therefore serving the Word and also walking in step with the Spirit so that the Word could be received, understood and become transformative in people's lives. Truth, new life and power are three characteristics of the work of the Spirit, but are also three moments in the life of faith in responding to the Gospel. These three are also especially relevant to the realities of digital culture today. An awareness of these infuses potential, hope and possibility into the way the Church of the future might take shape in serving and transforming the world.

II Authenticity and the Spirit of Truth

In his 2018 World Communications Day Message, Pope Francis decided to tackle one increasingly disturbing trend in social communications: the frequent emergence and spread of fake news, especially in and through social media.[2] In his warnings against the effects of the fake news phenomenon, he exhorts us to be purified by the truth in such a way that 'we discern everything that encourages communion and promotes goodness from whatever instead tends to isolate, divide, oppose. Truth therefore is not really grasped when it is imposed from without as something impersonal, but only when it flows from free relationships between persons, from listening to one another.'[3] Truth is unitive, it forges communion, it is relational, and it is found in authentic communication as a free and mutual sharing between persons. Although Pope Francis does not name it such, the description here for truth resonates deeply with the Holy Spirit. Recalling the description of the Spirit as a trinitarian bond of gift and love that exists between the Father and the Son, concepts like communion, mutuality and interpersonal bond all have pneumatological foundations.[4] As Francis continues to describe truth, the allusion to the Spirit continues. For example, he notes that 'we can recognize the truth of statements from their fruits: whether they provoke quarrels, foment division, encourage resignation; or on the other hand they promote informed and mature reflection leading to constructive dialogue and fruitful results.'[5] This brings to mind the Holy Spirit, particularly the fruits of the Spirit as listed in Galatians 5:22-23.

The connection between the Holy Spirit and truth is established in the tradition. Jesus refers to the Holy Spirit as 'the Spirit of Truth who will guide you into all the truth' in the Gospel of John and this title becomes part of the theological tradition.[6] As John Paul II discusses the Spirit of Truth in his 1986 encyclical *Dominum et Vivificantem*, he connects truth with faith: 'the guiding into all the truth is therefore achieved in faith and through faith: and this is the work of the Spirit of truth and the result of his action in man. Here the Holy Spirit is to be man's supreme guide and the light of the human spirit.'[7]

As the Spirit of Truth, the Spirit works to reveal to us the Word so that we can understand and respond in faith. This revelatory process is also a process infused with communication, human and divine. As the Church continues to read the signs of the times in the digital age, the need for truth vis-à-vis the problem of fake news is a surface level sign of a much greater challenge and opportunity. As people living in a digital culture, do we retain the capacity to see reality for what it is? Can we remain open to be addressed by the Word in a way that our words (and sounds and images on the screen) reflect its Good News? Can we discern truth so as to have life and live it abundantly? The Church of the future, sharing the Good News in digital culture, has the opportunity to offer a witness to the truth, as inspired by the Spirit, and to recall not only its content but worth and value for living well as a society.

Fake news is but one symptom of the greater issue of the struggle for authenticity in the digital age. The rapid and mediated flow of communication allows for the easy conveyance not only of bits of fake news but for systematic dishonesty, propaganda and disinformation which have broader effects in shaping or manipulating a cultural narrative. On an interpersonal level, this foments a lack of dialogue, closed mentality, intolerance and potential violence. It also normalizes the tendency to separate what is being communicated from actual reality. This can manifest in social propaganda or simply in a false but happier, thinner, more popular image of oneself projected on social media. In either case, we lose trust in what is being shared, which is detrimental to authentic communication. If true communication is rooted in the mutual self-gift offered in love of the Triune God as it unfolds among the divine persons, a basic lack of trust in the truthfulness of human communication is deeply problematic.[8] The lack of trust is a roadblock to receptivity, a roadblock to sharing and mutuality, and ruptures the basic bond that communication is built upon. Recalling Pope Francis' words above, this is the path to division and isolation rather than communion. The Holy Spirit as the Spirit of truth and as the bond of Gift and Love that makes all love and gifting possible for us is sorely needed in context. Part of the task of the future Church led by the Spirit then is to witness truth as it emerges in and through gift and love, and leads toward communion with God and one another.

III Words of Spirit and life

There is an integral connection between truth, communion and life. The Holy Spirit's guidance into all the truth is a guidance back toward communion with God, which ultimately is eternal life. When we recognize reality for what it is, we also recognize that which keeps us estranged, isolated or apart from God, self, and others. It is the work of the Spirit in this regard then to not only reveal the truth but guide us back to communion, by grace overcoming that which keeps us separated. The Spirit's work is therefore always uniting, bonding, reconciling, healing and life-giving. As the Spirit illuminates for us the Word in the process of revelation, this illumination always has a dynamism toward communion. Animated by the Spirit, the Church's work of proclaiming the Gospel should also carry this uniting, bonding, healing and life-giving work activity.

One of the challenges experienced in digital culture is the breaking of social bonds, isolation and estrangement that can emerge. In a cultural context built around connectivity, this challenge is a surprising one. We have all the technological means available to us to establish connections amongst ourselves, and these connections should carry the potential to deepen into or to strengthen already existing relationships. Communication in and through the digital networks has the potential to be oriented toward a sense of communion, both in a temporal sense but also heralding eternal communion with God.

At the same time, connections do not automatically become anything more profound than just connections, and these connections can be experienced in a way that is the opposite of communion: depersonalized responses or reactions to words on a screen, *ad hominem* attacks that do not take into consideration the dignity of the other, verbal harassment, threats, cyber bullying. Part of the relative anonymity of the screen allows for the emergence of these kinds of heightened responses, which are less likely to manifest as quickly and as strongly if two persons were meeting face to face rather than mediated by a screen. In any given comment feed we can see this occurring: a thread of comments quickly escalating from a difference of opinions to name-calling, sarcasm, harsh words, strong emotions. One wonders about the outcome of such battles, which result less in a true exchange of different perspectives and the possibility or learning something new, and more so in anger, embarrassment, tribalism and the reinforcement of previously held ideas.

Openness to communion assumes an openness to that which is outside of ourselves. If connections remain a sounding board for one's own ideas, this potential toward communion is hindered. It is the prophetic task of the Church to recall this potential toward communion, and to be a witness of open, listening, dialogical, mutual encounters in and through social communication. Instead of allowing the screen to function as a mirror that simply reflects back that which a person brings to it, the screen needs to remain a meeting point, a true mediator that reveals the possibility that there is much more to the persons who are posting or sharing particular bits of information there. There is always a full, dignified, contextual person behind the screen, and our social communication practices are in jeopardy if we forget this truth. As Pope Francis reminds us: 'the digital world is a network not of wires but of people.'[9] When we forget that there is a person behind the screen, it becomes easier to post flippant, sarcastic or hurtful words that lack the generosity of considering the dignity of the other.

Words that tear down, attack or hurt are fundamentally at odds with God's revelatory Word and Spirit. The Spirit who guides us into all the truth is also the Lord and Giver of Life as we profess in the Nicene-Constantinopolitan Creed. God's Word and Spirit are life-giving: they create, animate, restore, resuscitate and ultimately call toward eternal life with God. Whenever our own words fail to be life-giving to others, they also fall short of expressing authentic communication performed in the image of the Triune God: a gift of self, offered in love. Instead of harsh or cutting words, might we achieve making the same point in a way that offers possibility, hope, encouragement, and ultimately, the Good News to another person? In this we would be walking more in step with the Spirit who is Lord and Giver of Life. The future Church of the digital age might be especially attentive to standing as a witness to communication that is committed to be life-giving in this regard.

IV Authority and the power of the Holy Spirit

In early 2018, Facebook announced that it would shift what appears in the news feed away from showing postings by brands and companies and more toward postings by friends and family. In their own words, they instituted this change because they wanted to encourage more meaningful interactions among people.[10] Although seemingly a positive rationale, the company drew both suspicion and criticism for this shift. By changing the news feed, Facebook would change what information reaches people most readily, and many bristled at the obvious imposition of power and authority

Facebook was demonstrating, even if toward an arguably positive end.

In our digital culture, new expressions of authority have emerged alongside traditional forms and these new expressions sometimes challenge what we have known and accepted as authoritative before. One significant ground for the exercise of authority is the process by which information reaches us, especially the selection of information and the order in which information is ranked or presented. Because of the vast amount of information available in and through digital networks, media companies rely on algorithms to rank and sort the information that reaches a particular user. What we see in a news feed or search engine result page is not at all random, but has already been sifted, ranked, arranged, and sometimes sold and bought to appear before us and get our attention. The power to determine what information appears and what does not to a particular media consumer is significant power, lending new authority to Facebook, Google, Amazon, Netflix and similar companies. A critical question to pose about their authority is how much the information shown reflects the actual activity of people using the platforms, and how much of it is pre-determined by the values and assumptions of the people behind these platforms.

A simple example is the phenomenon of 'trending', whereby relevance is measured according to the frequency of popular engagement with the topic of a posting. Yet, what is the process by which a platform determines what trends? Algorithms have a mysterious reputation, and the answer to how much a company like Facebook promotes certain values or points of view is ambiguous. In this context, a consumer might rightly wonder not only if the information retrieved is fake news, but also whether it carries an agenda, and whose agenda this is. This, too, introduces a level or mistrust into the process of social communication.

Where do we encounter the Holy Spirit in this and how can the Church address this shifting expression of authority with the Gospel? Our language of describing the Holy Spirit often includes reference to the Spirit's power. We make reference to divine action and human action responding to grace all performed 'by the power of the Holy Spirit'. Yet, as paragraph 687 of the Catechism describes the Spirit's agency, it is a 'proper divine self-effacement' of the Spirit who 'reveals God, makes known to us Christ, his living Utterance, but the Spirit does not speak of himself.' In this light, the power of the Holy Spirit is far from the kind of worldly or self-aggrandizing power that wields forceful authority over the weaker. The power of the Holy Spirit is instead a power of self-gift that is extended to draw us into the bond of divine love. Here, too, we return to the theological notion of communication as self-gift offered in love and to the Holy Spirit as both the love and the gift, and the agent of all loving and gifting. Power and authority as revealed by Word and Spirit convey the unexpected: humility, self-emptying, sacrifice, the cross. As expressions of authority and power over information continue to shift in the digital world, divine power and authority revealed to us as self-gift brings a profound reminder that there is another way to exercise these concepts. On the more practical level, imagining how self-gift would manifest in social communication is a salient exercise, especially concerning how it would provide a counter-example to or displace self-promotion and the agenda-driven sharing of information. A prophetic task of the future Church would be to witness what self-gift can look like in digital communication practices.

V Conclusion

The Church is never apart from the work of the Spirit. As we imagine the future Church sharing the Gospel in digital culture, discerning how the Spirit moves in Church and in culture is essential. This essay sought to name some tension points that have surfaced in digital culture, suggesting connections to Word, Spirit and the tasks of a future Church along the way. Truth, authority and life in this light are not just tension points but three areas of hope and possibility where a pro-active Church can do excellent work already today.

Notes

1. Mark 16:15.
2. Francis, 'The Truth Will Set You Free (Jn 8:32): Fake News and Journalism for Peace'. Message of His Holiness Pope Francis For World Communications Day. 24 January 2018. https://w2.vatican.va/content/francesco/en/messages/communications/documents/papa-francesco_20180124_messaggio-comunicazioni-sociali.html.
3. Francis, 'The Truth Will Set You Free'.
4. See for discussion on the Holy Spirit as Gift and Love paragraph 10 in John Paul II, *Dominum et Vivificantem*. 18 May 1986. http://w2.vatican.va/content/john-paul-ii/en/encyclicals/documents/hf_jp-ii_enc_18051986_dominum-et-vivificantem.html.
5. Francis, 'The Truth Will Set You Free'.
6. John 16:13; Catechism of the Catholic Church, no. 692.
7. John Paul II, *Dominum et Vivificantem*, 6.
8. For the definition of communication as a divine gift of self offered in love, see paragraph 11 in Pontifical Council for Social Communication, *Communio et Progressio*. 23 May 1971. http://www.vatican.va/roman_curia/pontifical_councils/pccs/documents/rc_pc_pccs_doc_23051971_communio_en.html.
9. Francis, 'Communication at the Service of an Authentic Culture of Encounter'. Message of Pope Francis for the 48th World Communications Day. 24 January 2014. http://w2.vatican.va/content/francesco/en/messages/communications/documents/papa-francesco_20140124_messaggio-comunicazioni-sociali.html.
10. A. Mosseri, 'News Feed FYI: Bringing People Closer Together'. 11 January 2018. https://newsroom.fb.com/news/2018/01/news-feed-fyi-bringing-people-closer-together/

Part Four: The Keystone

Listening: the Path to Salvation and to the Transformation of the Church

THIERRY- MARIE COURAU

We live in a time when salvation seems to be an idea which is far removed from any contemporary reality. To envisage the Church of the future we must make sure that salvation, which is given in Christ and which the Church proclaims, is credible and accessible in people's lives. This requires a theological and pastoral work which begins with the experience of the suffering of the poor and by looking through the eyes of the poor. It is necessary for us to put ourselves in an attitude of listening, of obedience. The word 'listening' does not belong in usual theological discourse. Yet sin finds its origins specifically in a failure to listen. Listening to the words which God Himself speaks, which are inseparable from the actions He takes, is the gateway to a true understanding of salvation, which for the Church is the universal sacrament. The Church must be inspired and transformed by the life of the Spirit in the here and now.

To envisage the Church of the future, we must first envisage its mission. 'All renewal in the Church must focus on mission, so as not to fall into the trap of being a Church centred on itself.'[1] Making salvation accessible to all is a continuation of the work of Christ, as is making the Church accessible to all. Today, the Church and its discourse appears more and more esoteric and strange to many, especially in secularised Western countries or in areas where Christians are in the minority. Even in regions which remain Christian, few are able to give meaning to the term 'salvation' in a way which seems generally acceptable. We live in a time when it is difficult to think of 'heaven and hell' in Christianity – the afterlife, but also sacrifice,

113

redemption, atonement, resurrection, even forgiveness and reconciliation. Salvation seems to be an idea which is far removed from all contemporary reality, a forgotten idea. Nowadays, the search for healing for people and societies, or for well-being, has become the main object, including in religious circles. The word 'salvation' is helpful in liturgy insofar as it allows for a common vocabulary through which the paschal mystery and the community which it creates can be experienced; however, the meaning of the word remains unclear. The concept of the salvation of the world lives on but it is disembodied, without any real impact on people's lives. And yet, without a vision of salvation which is understandable and sufficiently meaningful to the lives of contemporary communities, there is no Church.

To envisage the Church of the future, therefore, it is necessary to re-examine the roots of what the Church needs to be in order to fulfil its mission, which is to open the doors of 'being just and good' to all. This in turn will lead to a renewal of pastoral life, preaching, mission, and commitment to justice. The salvation made available in Christ which the Church proclaims, and which is always available, must be believable and visible in the lives of individuals and groups- in the lives of all people. Pathways and experiences which lead people into the life of the Kingdom must be available in the real world, here and now, just as Christ announces: 'The time has come... the kingdom of God is near' (Mark 1: 15)'. This puts the Church in a state of transformation (*metanoia*), and of conversion (Matt 3:2) and demands a process of serious theological and pastoral work so it can be understood by ministers. Salvation can then be offered and explained to the modern world as a reality which people can access, and which can transform their daily lives, leading them step by step into a life of goodness, right in the midst of the diverse world they live in.

I The cries of the world are the beginnings of salvation

How can we re-imagine salvation if we do not first experience the perspective of those who, 'having no other servant than themselves (Henri-Dominique Lacordaire)', are in an unconscious waiting, an inexpressible desire for someone to release them, save them, find them, serve them. The true poor are those who struggle to survive, even if their groans are silent, and even if their poverty is not material. The true poor are buried by their cry, by their complaint, hoping for a new life. 'The reality of being poor can be summed up in one word: it is a cry that crosses the heavens and reaches God. What is the cry of the poor, if not one of suffering and loneliness, disappointment and hope?'[2] Often, most often, their experience is that no one around them hears or sees them. For society, they do not exist. They are outside of the supportive networks that the dominant groups have built. The Jewish faith and the Christian faith, however, attest that God hears the cries of the poor. Having heard them, he sees that they are trapped and intervenes. In the first Covenant, there are abundant examples of a God who intervenes to liberate, beginning with the release of the Hebrews in Egypt. 'He has shown strength with his arm.; he has scattered the proud in the thoughts of their hearts' (Lk 1: 51). His living power dwells in them from that point. It is thus that the people of God, these people, recognise themselves as being released by the force of the Living Word, by the spoken act of God.[3] 'Blessed are you who are poor, for yours is the Kingdom of God' (Luke 6:20). The Word of God enters humanity through the poor, and because of them. He finds in Mary- the ultimate descendant in a line of suffering poor (*anawim*) in God, waiting for the liberation of Israel – the space capable of receiving him. Jesus is the Father's answer to the cry. God makes himself a suppliant among humanity, renouncing the majesty of his divinity, in order to learn from and with human beings how to pass through death with his power of life, bringing with him into life all those who follow him. Through Jesus, through being human, God sees, hears and knows the world of the poor, and leads them to a good life. His project for the salvation of suffering humanity is made possible through them.

To experience life in the suffering and through the eyes of the poor is revealed as necessary for the Church to be Christlike. This choice of behaviour requires us to be in an attitude of listening, of obedience. This word, which is often misunderstood as submission, must be understood according to the New Testament Greek, which expresses the act of listening, of placing ourselves in a listening frame of mind. The Church, by understanding that it only becomes itself in obedience to God, is called to allow itself to be renewed through the realisation that this means it must obey those who are truly poor. In other words, the Church must put itself at the feet of the poor (John 13: 14-17), to see and understand with their feet and their arms, to discern from their experience, their day to day life. Pope Francis opens the way for a new model of Church, rooted in the path of the poor, who are models for the Kingdom.

In the eyes of the world they are of little value, and yet they are the ones who open the way to heaven, they are our 'passports to paradise'. For us, it is an evangelical duty to take care of them- they who are our true wealth – and to do it not only by giving them bread, but also by breaking open the bread of the Word with them, as they are the Word's most natural recipients.[4]

All this is not of a different nature to the liturgy of salvation which the Church celebrates daily in prayer, in which we listen to God and to humanity in order to live out the work of salvation accomplished by Christ. However, it appears that this other dimension of listening is secondary, even forgotten, by many Christians. Perhaps it is just poorly understood- reduced to a method of mental and spiritual accompaniment, or simply to a more efficient pastoral ministry.

The word 'listening' does not belong in normal theological discourse, neither does the word dialogue, which is only seen as theological from a certain disposition of the heart and of intelligence. This absence in contemporary theology has some parallels with the disappearance of the true meaning of the word salvation. If the story of the liberation of the Hebrews begins with God listening to their cries, God, in turn, asks his people to listen to him, if they want life. *Shema*, Israel! (Deut. 6:4). Without listening, there is no salvation. Without listening to the cries of the world, without listening to Scripture and to the poor, without listening to those who form the Church in its plurality of cultures and personal and collective stories, without listening to those damaged by the practice and words of its members, without listening to women, without listening to the sister Churches, without listening to the religious traditions of the world, without listening to societies, without listening to nature, the Church cannot respond to the proclamation of salvation by God the Trinity in Christ, from whom it receives its life and mission.

II A failure to listen, the destruction of relationship

It is legitimate from a theological point of view to emphasise listening in the work of salvation, because sin can also find its origin in a failure to listen.[5] The process by which sin unfolds itself is rooted in bad listening, in false hearing- partial, and harmed by the ambition to succeed by oneself. In the mythical and symbolic story of the fall of Adam and Eve in the book of Genesis (2-3), we are told of this failure to listen, from which Augustine derives the idea of original sin.[6] To rely only on one's own ability to hear, to close one's ears, to compose a lie made up of two separate truths, to be seduced by lies, to silence those who speak the truth: all these acts testify to the greatest temptation of humanity – letting ourselves be led by a desire for domination rather than listening to the cries of the oppressed and working with them to form a joyful community of brothers. In modern international societies, money has become the idol to which we must submit in order to satisfy our appetites. It shores up a system which allows the unlimited enjoyment of one group, which goes as far as to voluntarily humiliate the weak, while controlling and suppressing words which speak the truth. The gospels are full of examples of this in the parables of Jesus – the eldest son of the prodigal father, the Pharisee and the tax collector, etc. – and also in the description of those who seek to trap him and get rid of him- the accusers of the adulterous woman, the Sadducees, etc.

In the contemporary world ruled by technology and science, the ongoing societal crises come primarily from the ever-present games of power and control which arise in particular from the kind of money that has become all-embracing, perverse and untouchable, even for the governments which are trying to be democratic. These governments require the establishment of relationships of trust between citizens and those in power, based on listening and dialogue. The power which is given over to money feeds a lack of trust in those relationships.[7] Confidence in the future is linked to the accumulated worth of goods, and no longer in the quality of relationships (Luke 12: 13-21). This kind of wealth isolates and does not see the poor anymore. Trust between humans is gradually being destroyed and is being replaced by a continuous series of lies about reality, by a moral blindness which is devoid of guilt.

In the modern world, this affects our entire planet. Countless riches appear to be available, accessible to the most grasping and the most determined. The risk today is that we might enslave ourselves, in a similar way to the time of Europeans discovering the 'new worlds' in the last millennium, when people and gold were trafficked and submission to this game was the only reasonable course allowed. The same was true with industrialisation, with the power of the atom, etc. Those who accumulate wealth protect themselves but exclude and reject others. Submission to Mammon leads to confusion, violence, division, destruction and death. For Jesus, the rich man who does not hear and see the poor man who is at his door excludes himself from a part of his humanity, and therefore from his life too. This is definitive as well. He creates a vacuum of justice and therefore loses himself (Luke 16: 19-30). As for the poor man, God sees and hears his cry. He will be restored in the eyes of all to the self which he never lost to begin with. This lesson commands us to bring into being a just future (Matt 6:24).

III The transformation of the Church: choosing the act of listening time and again

The Church, which must love this world as God loves it and must want to take care of it, must be ever more vigilant of the evil games in which it can itself be trapped too. It must choose again and again to stand with humanity on the road to salvation. This is the Church's *metanoia*, which it must always take up. This Gospel term expresses the need to constantly renew one's way of seeing by the leading of the Spirit.

It is therefore necessary not only to renew the old, but also to allow the Holy Spirit to create something new. Not us: the Holy Spirit. To make room for the Holy Spirit, to allow the Holy Spirit to create new things, is to make all things new (see Ps 104: 30, Matt 9: 17, 2 Ph 3: 13, Rev 21: 5). The Spirit is the chief protagonist of the mission: she is the 'executive officer' of the pontifical works of mission. It's her, not us. Do not be afraid of the new things that come from the crucified and risen Lord: these novelties are beautiful.[8]

The Church must constantly re-adjust its understanding of the life of the world because the world is ever-changing. Today, this is happening at an even faster rate. The Church can only achieve this by being like God and listening to the world. God listens by being on the same level as the world and as suffering humanity. For Jesus, this is carried through even until death on the cross alongside a thief who asks for salvation. Listening changes our way of seeing, it converts us. When the Church chooses to listen to the poor, it chooses to be converted by God. Not only does it then invest in relieving and repairing real situations of poverty (slavery, migrants, the homeless, women, etc.), but it also puts into practice the wisdom received from Christ in order to reduce the structures of sin which generate misery, indignity and the death of relationship. This leads to the social doctrine it promotes and its concrete commitments to justice on the ground. The Church becomes prophetic when it allows itself to changed by that truth which sanctifies; the truth which works critically and hermeneutically on the very life of the Church so that it can be more how God wants it to be today for humanity. This creates paradigm shifts- not just a retreat to previous false paths- because it allows us to see things differently, out of the ordinary. This dynamism puts the Church in a situation of permanent *aggiornamento* (updating), to use the term given by Pope John XXIII for the Council and implemented by Pope Paul VI. In other words, its renewal can come only through poverty and charity,[9] by faith. For Jesus, to do the work of the Father is to believe in the One who sent him (John 6:29). The Spirit acts and leads on a people who are attentively listening, by faith. They thus becomes a prophetic people, where the new ways of love, presence, action, and the will of God are revealed and His work of salvation is revealed.

Listening is not easy for a Church which is institutionalised, because it is a source of authority in the eyes of many. And, like all those in power, it must resist the temptation to dominate rather than serve, to shut itself off and protect itself rather than to live out the truth. The recent example of the moral disaster of the Church of Chile and its hierarchy, highlighted by Pope Francis, shows how a contemporary national church can endanger the Church's proclamation of salvation by its refusal to listen. Hierarchies and clergy, especially but not only Roman Catholic ones, can allow themselves to be counterfeits of a willingness to listen to the calls of the world and the Spirit. Two examples in October 2018 can encourage the Church to resolutely take the path of learning how to listen. Pope Francis will canonise Pope Paul VI, who died on the Feast of the Transfiguration on August 6, 1964, and Oscar Romero, the Archbishop of San Salvador, who was murdered while giving a sermon on March 24, 1980. By bringing them forward for canonisation together, the Roman pontiff is associating the person who emphasised- throughout his ecclesiastical career and his pontificate- the necessity of dialogue between the Church and the world, with the person who became the defender of the poorest and whose voice and life was crushed by the most powerful. Both of them spoke words which directly addressed the importance of relationship within the question of salvation. Paul VI envisaged the history of salvation as a 'dialogue of salvation (ES)'. It requires us to enter into a life of listening which is nothing less than a life shared with the poorest. 'We must pursue a common purpose- provided these purposes are human and honest- especially with the least important, if we want to be listened to and understood. It is necessary- even before speaking- to listen to the voice and, even more importantly, to the heart of humanity; to understand it' (ES 90). Romero was aware of this even up to his time of death.

Authentic listening engages the listener, who does not know how to be passive. The listener is always in active mode. Being a disciple, a brother, sister, or even the mother of Christ, requires us to 'listen and put into practice' both his word and his actions (Lk 8:21). Active – because in its attention and movement towards others who speak, it is a choice, a decision to love and act for justice whatever the cost. Listening, which moves to action, is the way the Church works for justice in the world.[10] The term 'listening-action' can be used to emphasise the two-faceted work of salvation in which the Church participates. Attentively listening to Christ as master, the Church is then able to listen to all of reality with which it comes into contact. Christ listens to the Father. God listens the world. He hears the cries of the people, the cries of the poor, and He acts. He saves. Christ is the Logos made flesh. The Greek word *logos* comes from the verb *legein* which means specifically to gather words together before speaking. Gathering the cries of the world is the perfect work of the divine *logos*. In God, the Word is listening to the world. Christ in all his life and death shows how he is both listening to the Father and listening to the world, part of God and part of humanity. He allows the words (*logoi*) of humanity to pass through (*dia-*) him: *dia-logoi*. These words influence him and reveal to him the depth and the breadth of his mission (see the meeting with the Canaanite woman, Mt 15: 21-28). Through his resurrection, his willingness to receive the life of the Father by his complete obedience is made manifest, because of the very giving up of his life and placing of it into the hands of human beings and of the Father. His saving obedience is visible in the total surrender of himself in the act of listening, through which he accomplishes the work of justice. The Church, which continues the work of Christ in the world, cannot be or act differently from him. It has to adopt the Christ-like attitude of obedience to the Father, listening to the Father by listening to the poor. This is how the Church becomes the body of Christ.

Today, listening which must lead to justice is required for the Church in the service of every diverse grouping: young people (25% of the world population), the excluded in all kinds of societies (due to cultures of waste,[11] rejection, and contempt), the religious traditions of the world (a concentration of humanity's desire for salvation), and the planet (wounded, bruised, exploited). To listen to them is to be available to the life of the Spirit, to the dynamics of change, and to respond to the salvation that is coming, which leads Christians to seek and promote justice for every person and peace for all peoples, and to exercise the authority entrusted to us in the service of the communion of diversity.

Finally, if the listening-action is the gateway to a true understanding of salvation, the Church must adopt it more and more in its own inner life. Pope Paul VI endorsed this perspective when he created an international council around him, the Synod of Bishops.[12] He highlighted the importance of a collegial, participative and inclusive method of working, to advise and support the Roman pontiff. Pope Francis is continuing in this direction. Dialogical practice was used in the establishment of a council of nine cardinals, but even more significantly, it was put into practice for the very purpose of the development of doctrine, when it was implemented during the Synod on the family which lasted two years. Where it was customary to control discussion in order to maintain an ideological status quo, the Pope liberated it by making it possible on many levels: dioceses, institutions, bishops, invited members, etc. A genuine listening process has opened up new horizons that are more authentically evangelical and missionary. It has thus put a truly Synodical Church back on track, one which listens, and which has a better understanding when it comes out of the experience of the poor.

IV Conclusion

The mission and the life of the Church are inseparable. They are ordained to carry out the work of salvation for humanity. All people, and especially the poorest, must be able to see that the Kingdom has come near to them in their daily lives. For this reason, the biblical and evangelical insistence on listening-action and dialogue must play a decisive theological role in contemporary soteriology and the different aspects of the Church in the future. In a world where the Church loses more and more, including – fortunately – its power over people's minds and bodies, its transformation will be made possible by being alongside the poorest and by engaging with them for justice. It will lose its dominant position in order to acquire the ability to see what God hears and wants, and to renew and adjust. It will then fulfil its prophetic calling.

Translated by Ruth Wilde

Notes

1. Jean-Paul II, Post-Synodal apostolic exhortation, *Ecclesia in Oceania*, 22nd November 2001, 19. Cited by Pope Francis, *Evangelii gaudium* 27.
2. Pope Francis, Address for the 2nd annual World Day of the Poor, 13th June 2018.
3. Gustavo Guttierez, *A Theology of Liberation,* Brussels, Lumen Vitae, 1974, pp.206-212.
4. Rafael Luciani, *Pope Francis and the Theology of the People*, New York, Orbis Books, 2017.
5. Pope Francis, Sermon for the first World Day of the Poor, 19th November 2017.
6. Benedict XVI, Post-Synodal apostolic letter *Verbum Domini*, 30th September 2018, 26.
7. Paul Ricoeur, *Evil, a Challenge to Philosophy and Theology.*
8. Congregation for the Doctrine of Faith and Dicastery for Promoting Integral Human Development, Oeconomicae et pecuniariae quaestiones. *Considerations for ethical discernment on certain aspects of the current economic and financial system*, 6th January 2018.
9. Pope Francis, Speech to the general assembly on pontifical missionary works, 1st June 2018.
10. Paul VI, Encyclical *Ecclesiam suam*, 6th August 1964, 56-58.
11. See for example: Pope Francis, *Sermon on the 4th May 2017* (Evangelising without proselytising, but through listening), *Angelus 17th July 2016* (The roots of peace are in the capacity to listen), *Sermon from the 25th June 2015* (Knowing how to listen, and acting from a basis of listening), *Prayer from the 24th November 2013* (Marie, a woman who listens).
12. Pope Francis, Encyclical *Laudato si'*, 18th June 2015, 22:43.

Part Five: Theological Forum

Theology and the American Academy of Religion

GERARD MANNION

In this article, I will offer some reflections on the place of Christian theology within the American Academy of Religion (AAR, i.e., North America). It is a fascinating organization without which theology worldwide today would be very different.

I The story of the American Academy of Religion

The Academy is the largest professional association or society for the study of religion in the world. The past and present of the AAR are both very much bound up with biblical scholarship in the United States. Its origins date back to 1909 and the foundation of the Association of Biblical Instructors in American Colleges and Secondary Schools, which, in 1922, became the National Association of Biblical Instructors, and, in 1963, the AAR. Some of the AAR's past presidents have been key figures in theology, church history and theological ethics, with a few originating from beyond the United States.

The AAR began to cooperate closely with the older Society of Biblical Literature (SBL), which was founded in 1888 and is the other largest professional society in North America (and so presently globally). From 1970 onwards the two associations have held a joint annual meeting (known as a conference or convention in other parts of the world) that has enabled the AAR meeting to develop from a small meeting accommodated in a single conference hotel to the 10,000 plus participants that now regularly attend.

But there have been divisions that have impacted theology and other approaches to the study of religion alike. The joint meetings of the SBL and AAR were interrupted by an unpopular separation between 2008 and 2011, when some voices on the AAR committee pushed through a motion to hold separate meetings (with dire logistical and financial consequences for all concerned, including publishers, many of whom could simply not afford to attend both exhibitions that take place as a key component of the joint annual meeting).

The separation was ideologically driven. So many members of either association had research and teaching interests that legitimately crossed over into those areas covered by the sister association. Consequently, many believed a secularist agenda pursued by some scholars of religion had forced through this largely unwelcome split (the membership of both societies voted overwhelmingly to reverse it,[1] never having been given the chance to vote on it coming into being in the first place).

The temporary separation of the two associations may be seen to be grounded in broader questions surrounding the identities of the disciplines gathered in them. The now long worn and tedious departmental, institutional and disciplinary 'clashes' between theology and 'religious studies' preoccupied many scholars in the mid to late 1970s and beyond into the later 90s and, in some places, beyond even that decade and, sadly, to this day. Thankfully, this 'debate' has largely been judged by history to have been, in many ways, unhelpful and even unnecessary, although some departments remain trapped in such binary oppositional thinking to this day. Some may (needlessly) have perceived it in terms of competition, some bought wholesale into the triumph of secularization theories (some of the leading pioneering theorists of which later and, in a self-deprecating fashion, mocked their younger selves' mistakes and arrogance, for example Peter Berger). It is fair to say that the boundary lines between theology and 'religious studies' had never been fixed or never could be. Neither is technically a single unified discipline in and of itself. Theology has, since its beginnings crossed over into, learned from and contributed and helped to give birth and sustenance to so many other disciplines.

Religious studies is really an umbrella term that emerged in the 1960s and beyond, partly to reflect the impact of the many social scientific and related approaches to the study of religion that had emerged from the nineteenth century onwards. A second influential factor in the emergence

126

of Religious Studies departments was due to the fact that, in the United States, confessional theology could not receive state funding due to the constitutional separation of religion and state. Yet a new approach to the study of religion, one not formally linked to any particular faith community or religious institution, presented no such obstacles to funding by the state. This was something especially exploited in the University of California system, many constituent schools of which became pioneers in the study of religion, continuing such important work to this day.

But a third reason why divisions and debates occurred was because sometimes people were simply unaware of what their colleagues were doing in the perceived other yet clearly neighbouring, indeed often overlapping field. It is fair to say that there have always been theologians engaged in the study of religions other than their own and in methods beyond those technically identified as belonging to theology. And, especially since the late 1960s, many theologians have become increasingly conversant and interested in furthering the different methodologies for studying multiple religions that are core to religious studies. Many have happily lived and taught in both worlds, so to speak, advancing approaches across the divide. And so interreligious dialogue and religious pluralism have been greatly advanced thanks to this. The AAR has been a vital forum for allowing such cross-fertilization to take place and continues to be so.

As the organization grew, it is true that many theologians – including leading theologians – stopped attending the AAR at different points in the 1990s and especially early 2000s. There seemed to be an increasing reduction in program units focused upon core theological questions, and thus a lack of conference sessions, panels and papers that were of direct relevance to their work. Thankfully, such trends have been proactively reversed since the mid 2000s and theology is now either the primary focus or part of the major focus of a large proportion of the AAR's program units.

II Theological engagement through the Academy

So, what forms of theological focus take place through the work of the AAR? The annual meeting is the primary outlet for its work, yet the AAR does much more to foster scholarly enquiry. Alongside regular regional meetings, the Academy also publishes book series, awards various grants to facilitate and recognize scholarship and research (especially at earlier stages of careers), and it helps facilitate dialogue and research about religion-focused pedagogy and research themselves. Indeed, theology-oriented events have been some of the best-attended plenary sessions at the AAR in the past two decades, including an enormous audience turning out to attend a session about Pope Francis in Baltimore in 2013.

To name just a sampling of the program units that have advanced the discourse and practice of theology in recent decades, there are units that address Christianity as a whole from a variety of interdisciplinary methodological and geographical perspectives which are ecumenical in orientation and by deliberate design. So, for example, this present author can bear testimony to the aims of the Ecclesiological Investigations Program Unit, which is both linked to a much wider international network to promote open and pluralistic dialogue and scholarship about the church (especially ecumenical issues, interfaith issues, social justice and ethical issues and church-world/secular issues), and is a unit that has collaborated with other AAR groups each and every year since 2006. Similarly and since about the same time, the World Christianities Group has also taken a broad global sweep and explored this nascent new branch of theological focus from a wide variety of angles.

In addition to those groups with a firm commitment to exploring ecumenical issues, there are equally many which look at inter-religious issues and studies. Examples of those with the most direct focus on theological questions are the units in Comparative Theology, Comparative Religion Ethics and Contemplative Studies. Some groups explore specific ethical questions with a distinct commitment to theological approaches among the topics they discuss each year, such as the unit focusing on Class, Religion and Theology.

There are several denominational and tradition-specific units, such as the relatively recently introduced (2012) Vatican II Studies Unit and the Roman Catholic Studies Unit. Other denominations are covered by groups exploring Eastern Orthodox Studies, Lutheran, Reformed, Quaker and Methodist traditions. The Society for the Study of Anglicanism is presently an 'additional meeting group' which will hopefully be incorporated as a fully-fledged AAR group soon. Regional or country-specific attention is given in the recently formed Chinese Christianities Seminar and the unit on Middle Eastern Christianity.

And there is, of course, attention to the theologies of other traditions in various groups that focus on Daoism, Jainism, Islamic Studies, Jewish studies (and questions explored in an analogous fashion to those pursued through theological methods in Buddhist Studies).

There are groups which explore specific *methods* such as the section in Christian Systematic Theology in addition to units in Political Theology, Practical Theology, Liberation Theology, Feminist Theology, among other groups. Theological enquiry also receives much attention from historically oriented groups such as the History of Christianity Unit or the Nineteenth Century Studies. Some groups focus on prominent *standpoints* in recent times, e.g. Liberal Theologies and Open and Relational Theologies. And then there are groups that look at theology coming from particular communities and minorities. These include units in Black Theology, Queer Studies in Religion, and Indigenous Religious Traditions.

Some units explore the work and legacy of different theologians such as those exploring Augustine and Augustinianism, Barth, Kierkegaard, Tillich, Schleiermacher, Martin Luther King Jr., and others. Perhaps of significance, no single (modern) Roman Catholic theologian forms the focus of a dedicated group, perhaps reflecting the pluralism inherent in much Catholic theology, perhaps because Catholic scholars have yet to successfully propose one.

Theological questions also receive regular attention in the work of such groups that are either interdisciplinary by nature or by design such as Theology and Continental Philosophy or Theology and Religious Reflection.

III A European Academy of Religion begins

In June 2017, the very first annual conference of the newly founded European Academy of Religion (EUARE) was held in Bologna, Italy, where it met again in 2018. It will be fascinating to see the very different, yet, I am sure, complementary ways in which this initiative will further promote theological discourse and research long into the future. Its style is, of course, more European continental in approach and that variety and difference from the character of the AAR is a positive feature that offers a distinctive range of opportunities for theological scholarship today.

EUARE has begun with great promise and I have no doubt it will come to prove a very significant addition to the annual calendar of forums where both theology and all other approaches to the study of religion are discussed. Involvement by scholars from North America thus far has been obviously limited given various factors, not least of all practical and schedule-related ones, but, again, I am sure intercontinental conversations and collaboration in the study of theology and religion will benefit all the more for the presence of these two associations.

It is too early to provide a similar overview on EUARE to that which has been given above on the AAR, but perhaps it deserves one of its own to reflect its origins and beginnings already. In years to come, I am sure it will warrant a very significant assessment both in retrospective and prospective terms alike.

IV Academies of incomparable value for theology

The AAR is without parallel in the world. Yes, there are areas where it could be improved, and the schedule grows and becomes more relentlessly intensive each year. An additional day or so could profitably be added to its program. There is simply no annual gathering that offers so many opportunities for scholars to present their work, hear the work of others and to engage in a host of important meetings and networking opportunities of invaluable significance for their work and development alike. The enormous exhibition hall to which every single major and so many smaller publishers of theology come each year is itself a unique opportunity for scholars to explore the scholarship emerging in their fields of interest and to directly speak with publishers about future book projects they have in mind. Many journals, special interest groups and international and national networks host their own business meetings around the schedule of the AAR. The giants of the field can be heard and engaged with, alongside the most exciting emerging voices, too. Friends old and new encounter one another each November. It can sometimes feel as if anyone and everyone in the world of theology is there, despite some stubborn stay always deterred by the sheer size of the gathering or practical issues such as the not insignificant costs. Theology would be all the poorer and more limited in range and scope if the AAR did not exist. Now that we also have the EUARE, the future of theology looks all the brighter still.

Notes

1. Or, more accurately, to commit to simultaneous meetings open to both organizations' members in the same location each year.

Public Theology and Publishing
A Survey from the West
of Continental Europe

GIANLUCA MONTALDI AND PIER LUIGI CABRI

Theology may always have been a phenomenon open to the context in which it emerges, but only in recent times has the need been felt to formalise its public character in epistemological terms as well as others, in recognition of the pluralism within which this discipline is developing today. The brief discussion that follows is an attempt to outline the consequences of this for the field of theological publishing, at least in the West of the European continent.

I A glance at history

Our starting point is the flourishing of theological and religious publishing, at least from 1800, which brought into being various publishing houses.[1] Initially, production concentrated on works of a devotional or catechetical character, with a significant presence of texts on the bible; a few exceptions that had a more theological approach and had notable success were the lives of Jesus written by David Friedrich Strauss, (1835), François Mauriac (1836), Ernest Renan (1863) and Giovanni Papini (1921). A second phase was marked by the establishment of entrepreneurial denominational publishing, in Italy, for example, with the appearance of the Pia Società S. Paolo in 1914 and in 1918 of Vita e Pensiero. In the second part of the last century, a major focus of interest was the Second Vatican Council: this brought an intensification of publications and publishers, now inter-denominational and international and including various theological disciplines.

In the course of this recent history a number of tendencies have become dominant. On the level of *structures*, there have been a number of mergers; with few exceptions, where small publishing houses have maintained a niche production thanks to the support of a research institution, broader theological publishing has gradually been absorbed by the big publishing groups, which explains the disappearance of many publishing houses in various countries.[2] On the level of *production and distribution*, there has been a two-way movement: on the one hand, the 'lay' branch has opened to the publication of non-theological religious works; on the other, publishing houses with a history of religious publishing have invested in the production of popular narrative texts, and this process has been helped considerably by the development of integrated systems between different publishers backed by structural coordination. On the level of *content*, there has been an opening out to the world of religion in general and, in particular, to religious pluralism and syncretism; in response to the demands of the market, there has also been an increase in the publication of texts on the border between spiritual exploration and theological reflection. Finally, on the level of *language*, if publishing had already made a great contribution to the updating of theology by translations in individual languages, English has been adopted as the international lingua franca, especially for journals.

All these tendencies are transforming the European publishing market; and even if it is not all easy to guess whether they will continue, they are already determining the choice of subjects, of authors and readers, even in the publication of theological books. Moreover, we need to get beyond the idea – which Yves Congar denounced long ago! – of creating parallel structures for individual denominations and religions and the secular world. Accordingly, the impression of being right back at the beginning of Catholic publishing and religious publishing in general has some justification,[3] and invites us to leave our comfort zone and find the courage to make choices in favour of quality rather than our niche. In fact, 'in only a few years in Italy the readership of religious books has more than doubled from 2,700,000 in 2010 to 5,700,000 today, though the presence of secular publishers in the sector is increasing,' and readers are getting younger and more demanding.[4]

134

II Tendencies in theology

Alongside the change in the editorial style of theological publishing, proposals have been put forward for a change in theology itself. In any case, every period has in some sense concentrated on specific forms of publishing: the commentaries on the Church fathers, the medieval *summae*, and the manuals of the modern period in a way reflected the spirit of their time, and perhaps the co-authored 'study' is gradually becoming typical of recent decades. This is reflected in a theology that tends no longer to encourage the construction of individual academic systems, but to a taking on of new questions, to the reformulation of topics and the bringing together of different viewpoints. Not without reason has it been suggested that the 'new' theology should be reinterpreted as a change of style, and even regarded as the style (C. Theobald, E. Salmann), and in this phase the new political theology (J.B. Metz) has still much to offer.

This reconstruction may be aided by new theological institutions at a European level. The main examples are the Catholic Society for Theology, the European Academy of Religion and the chairs of the history of Christianity or inter-religious dialogue. The first, founded in 1989, has the goal of promoting the academic study of theology at the interface of Church experience and society, and two key aims are to cross national boundaries and to look for young authors. The aim of the second, newer and more ambitious, is to help to create a common understanding of the importance of religious pluralism, religious freedom, ecumenical dialogue and the role of religions in creating peace and civil society in a global world. The last two could become the beginning of a new vocation for Europe, creating a secular society that is also able to speak the language of religious pluralism, a secular culture that does not exclude, but welcomes, dialogue.

III Theology 2.0

The introduction of digital production into publishing has meant not only an adjustment in the appearance of texts (e-books or e-zines), but has also had an impact on sales methods and even on the perception of the work and its author, to the point of putting at risk the modern systems of copyright protection. In addition, a recent study on literary competence in Europe has shown that the younger generations have increasingly less difficulty in reading online texts,[5] while on average only 40% of the population (in Italy) read at least one book a year. All this ought to make it clear that the theological publishing market may be expected to continue to move into digital production.

The first step is to make texts from the theological tradition accessible in a new way and more widely available. The bible is already widely available on the internet: the site *NT Gateway*, for example, managed by Mark Goodacre, offers an annotated list of the main resources for the study of the main New Testament problems,[6] and there are also now digital editions of the bible available to all. More narrowly focused sources are Intratext or the *Post-Reformation Digital Library*, where texts from the worldwide Catholic and Protestant theological traditions can be accessed.[7] In addition, there needs to be a greater effort to promote the sale of theological products online, since the percentage of theology sold in the secular online market (12.95%) is almost the same as that in the religious market (16.50%).

Nevertheless, we should be missing the point if we remained fixated on the formal diversity of what is published. In reality, what is needed is a change of mindset as regards the work accomplished to date. As A. Del Maso acutely noted in his 2017 comments on the annual report of the UELCI Observatory on religious publishing, precisely because of the transformations mentioned in this article, our effort must be directed to quality publications that arouse the interest of readers of the second millennium.[8] The dead weight of post-conciliar theology and the inability of the denominational publishing firms to do anything new – they are often tied into clerical choices and patrons who will always praise the publications – and sometimes oppose similar new developments, among other things because established names have difficulty in giving way to young authors and because they lack the courage to accept that the Church and religious world they have known is coming to an end, and so make only short-term plans. Moreover, young theologians are not always adequately trained, even theologically, to face public discussion, since their training is very often limited to internal Church – or even sacristy – questions. Successful exploration beyond these limits is what could be the key to the future of theological and religious publishing in Europe. We need to hear the prophetic words that helped this sector in 1800 and 1900:

'We should...all of us, women and men of goodwill, be more courageous, rejecting the small and large drugs that the market offers us, not accepting the blackmail of conventional answers, and becoming once more reactive and active, dissatisfied and demanding, starting in the field of ideas, study and thought. We must write and read what nourishes and awakens and not what justifies us and sends us to sleep.'[9]

Translated by Francis McDonagh

Notes

1. For Herder, cf K.-T. Humbach et al. (ed.), *Der Verlag Herder: 1801-2001 – chronologischer Abriss seiner Geschichte mit Synchronopse zum Geistes- und Weltgeschehen (200 Jahre Herder)*, Freiburg i. Br., 2001; for Éditions du Cerf, the recent study by É. Fouilloux, *Les éditions dominicaines du Cerf: 1918-1965*, Paris, 2018; for a short history of religious publishing in Italy, cf M. Roncalli – G. Vigini, *L'editoria religiosa in Italia. Contributi e materiali per una storia*, Napoli, 2009, and G. Vigini, S*toria dell'editoria cattolica in Italia. Dall'Unità ad oggi*, Milan, 2017; for Spain, cf J.L. Ruiz Sánchez (ed.), *Catolicismo y Comunicación en la Historia Contemporánea*, Santander, 2005.
2. A unique and significant case of this concentration, has been the decision of the Holy See to give the Libreria Editrice Vaticana the rights to all official papal documents: cf http://www.vatican.va/roman_curia/institutions_connected/lev/docs_lev/copyright_it.htm.
3. Cf R. Righetto, *Editoria cattolica all'anno zero*, in http://rivista.vitaepensiero.it/news-vp-plus-editoria-cattolica-allanno-zero-4886.html. Righetto's article provoked a variety of comments from denominational publishing in Italy: cf http://rivista.vitaepensiero.it/news-vp-plus-editoria-cattolica-allanno-zero-le-case-editrici-rispondono-4895.html; http://rivista.vitaepensiero.it//news-vp-plus-editoria-cattolica-allanno-zero-il-dibattito-continua-4904.html. The impression of being in the stone age seems to be strengthened by the news that the British and Foreign Bible Society started operating in Italy on 1 April 2018.
4. Cf M. Roncalli, *Ecco chi scriverà di religione nei prossimi anni e quali saranno i nuovi lettori*, in http://www.lastampa.it/2017/04/21/vaticaninsider/ita/inchieste-e-interviste/ecco-chi-scriver-di-religione-nei-prossimi-anni-e-quali-saranno-i-nuovi-lettori-2faXnP1owT69G4ov0xbJLO/pagina.html.
5. Cf http://timssandpirls.bc.edu/pirls2016/international-results/pirls/summary/.
6. Cf http://www.ntgateway.com.
7. Cf http://www.intratext.com/ and http://www.prdl.org/.
8. Cfr. A. dal Maso, *Il libro religioso: se realtà e fantasia sorpassano gli schemi. Verso una UELCI 2.0?*, in http://www.cittadellaeditrice.com/munera/chiesa-in-uscita-e-buona-stampa-una-vibrante-analisi-di-alberto-dal-maso/. UELCI is the association of Catholic publishers and bookshops in Italy and since 2001 has published an annual survey of the state of religious publishing.
9. G. Fofi, *Editoria cattolica: eppure si muove...*, in http://rivista.vitaepensiero.it//news-vp-plus-editoria-cattolica-eppur-si-muove-4921.html?

Humanae Vitae Fifty Years On:
The Meaning of an Anniversary

ANTONIO AUTIERO

The approaching 50th anniversary of Paul VI's Encyclical *Humanae Vitae* (25 July 1968) is giving rise to a series of initiatives, intense discussion, and also some controversy. The anniversary is being taken by different sides as an opportunity for completely contrasting purposes. There are those who express the desire to reiterate the doctrine expressed in that Encyclical in rejecting the moral lawfulness of recourse to contraception. There are those who would opt for a 're-writing' of the Encyclical, in the light of more recent doctrinal and pastoral developments. There are also many who would see a shift of emphasis in conjugal and sexual morality as being an appropriate attitude, no longer focussing so acutely on the specific problem of contraception.

In reality, the variety of positions reveals a diversity of options, with regard to a broader theological and ecclesial scenario which for some must go back to the inter-weaving between the text of the Encyclical and the context of the teaching of the Second Vatican Council. For some groups, on the other hand, the 50th anniversary of *Humanae Vitae* (*HV*) is an opportunity to 'settle things' with the Church's current leadership, in a summary judgment of the pontificate of Francis and the leanings of those episcopates and theologians closest to it.

We cannot not view the temptation and attempt to use the Encyclical's anniversary 'politically', as though in the materiality of its doctrinal position it must be considered to be a criterion for evaluating the truth and a judgement of the orthodoxy of believers, pastors, theologians, and the simple faithful. While this might seem to be an aspiration which has increased in recent years, in reality we must acknowledge that precisely such a focus on adherence to *HV* has been a criterion of judgement over recent decades (particularly from 1970 to 1995). The genesis of a certain ethical fundamentalism, which emerged in the Catholic Church in precisely that period, cannot be understood without identifying specific attention towards issues of sexual ethics (and of contraception, in particular), also on the part of institutions checking and verifying the trustworthiness of individuals or groups with regard to their theological and ethical stances. As an example of all this, one can refer to the so-called 'Kölner Erklärung' (1989) and later to the 'Kirche 2011 – ein notwendiger Aufbruch' Memorandum. Even though both arose in German-speaking theological-ecclesial circles, they have had a much wider significance and generated an open attitude, conscious of the complexity of the problems and the need for reform.

In this article we intend to propose a starting point for reflection to be developed further, preferring a more openly 'hermeneutical' use of the anniversary rather than a political one. In other words, we want to indicate two paths to be pursued, to grasp the importance of the dynamic character of a moral teaching on the go. In reality, this attitude, with different nuances and intensities, concerns every doctrinal system and both guards against the risk of fossilizing it and the temptation to use it for regrettable ends; in either case, in the end, by betraying it.

I Re-contextualizing the genesis of *HV*

Over the last fifty years of the practice of the Christian life and the work of theological reflection, new contexts in which ethics operates, to which we can no longer close our eyes, have emerged. We will mention two explicitly. The first concerns the concept of nature, on which *HV* mainly focuses its reasoning. The second, obviously connected to the first, touches the horizon of the meaning and functions of human sexuality.

At the time *HV* was written, different motives led to the adopting of a concept of nature strongly conditioned by its biological (biologistic) character. Even though at the time there was no lack of open, more markedly anthropological approaches, *HV* nevertheless developed an ethical-normative reading linked to the deontological approach, whereby the criterion of conformity to nature, understood as the totality of intentionality and binding structures inscribed in the constitution of the human being and expressed in its biological functions, played a decisive role. In the wake of this, sexuality, too, was understood mainly in relation to its procreative function, obviously without denying the presence of other dimensions, such as the affective, relational, and social dimensions, but without assuming a vision of dynamic and differentiated unity which leads to an understanding of what is specifically human in the sexuality of the person.

Now, in considering the origins of *HV*, awareness of the intertwining of this dual perspective cannot be put to one side. Besides, this awareness of the stated limitations has synergistically guided both the magisterial activity of pastors (think, for example, of John Paul II's theology of the body) and the commitment of reflection and the development of theology. The contribution of human sciences in the extended sense is decisive and no longer revocable, in particular the contribution of philosophical and theological anthropology and of the biological and behavioural sciences.

What is more, over the same decades which comprise these 50 years of *HV*, a concept of nature which is recovering its ecological dimension, concerned with the scale of both the macrocosm (the universe and its survival) and the microcosm (the organism and its well-being), has been developing alongside the biologically crystallized concept of nature held tight in the grip of an essentialist-individualist view. Now it is precisely this broader viewpoint which enables understanding, from a different perspective, the importance of respect for the natural sphere and the urgency of not exposing the body to manipulative effects which can alter its equilibrium. So, it is not said that the rejection of recourse to contraceptive practices of a chemical nature (the pill) must go through the narrow and problematic system of the deontological-essentialist argument. To assume responsibility for one's own bodily sphere, to develop a true and proper ecology of the body can have in itself useful, productive elements, binding to guide the operative choice, with respect to the problem posed. But this goes back to the dynamic of responsible choice, which inevitably again places the person and their vision of life at the centre.

And on the sexuality front, the awareness of the de-centrality of the sexual act, in favour of the relational dynamic, where the sexuality of the couple becomes place and language, is of irrevocable importance. Now we must be mindful precisely of the culture developed by women in these same years of *HV*. It has made us sensitive to the risk of the manipulation of the female body to the advantage of male hoarding and domination. An unbalanced liberalization of the choice of pharmacological contraception does not exclude the risk of male domination, for which the female body pays the price; a price which, moreover, is demanded of women, even through the categorical rejection of contraception, delaying the processes of sex education as education of subject to responsibility. It can be well understood, therefore, that even through this culture which emerges from the stories of women and their awareness, the concept of nature acquires a more distinctly relational dimension and the view of sexuality is open to an intensification of humanising significance, critical with regard to dominating powers and full of energy of emancipation.

II Conscience, truth and history

A second path of reflection broadens, but does not divert from, the space of consideration. Precisely in the most recent discussions on the anniversary of *HV*, controversy often resurfaces among those who refer to the sincere experience of believing couples who have experienced or are living out the conflict between conscience and the norm contained in the Encyclical. For these careful readers and sensitive pastors, the consideration of the life story of so many believers is a source of knowledge about the truth of the norm itself which cannot be ignored. The opposite side gets irritated by this reproach, affirming the 'objective' truth of the norm, as content of magisterial pronouncement. The sum of the distress, even though assessable, does not, they say, undermine the moral truth of the norm.

The framework of this controversy makes us understand the need to reflect on two things. The first is that the so-called 'objective order' of the norm and presumed 'subjective leeway' of the individual and his/her conscience must be considered to be a category which equally impacts the theme of truth in the moral sphere. It is the 'truth of life' (*Veritas vitae* is an ancient term which dates back to Pope Adrian VI in the sixteenth century). Whoever reduces life to mere facticity, not correlated to its expressive capacity of that moral authenticity which emerges from lived history and from the reflected experience of believers, must pose the question of the meaning of moral truth, without confusing it with the truth of faith or, more generally, with theoretical truth. The confusion of the two levels reveals once again the essentialist matrix of the framework and leads to the demand the same dynamic of genesis and validation from practical truths as we would from speculative truths. To iron out on the same parameter practical reason and theoretical reason ignores not just a representative claim of the spirit of modernity (Kant), but distances itself from an understanding of Christian tradition expressed in the scholastic-medieval vision of Thomas Aquinas.

The second thing to be considered concerns the profound, creative and regenerating significance of the sensus fidelium. In knowing about things to do with faith and morals, the community of believers, in all its enunciations, is living out of an instinct of understanding and recognition that does not isolate one from the other, does not produce the formation of contrasting sides and does not entrust itself to logics of power and dominion. The *sensus fidelium* values experience which is authentically undertaken and circulated. Its expressions are sometimes more articulated and resonant, sometimes, on the other hand, it allows itself to be grasped by the subdued tones of those who suffer the conflict and do not even succeed in naming it.

It is not the quantitative, opinion-poll total of opinions, but the desire to listen to that truth which emerges from lived experience to make us understand not just the opportunity, but also the duty to understand differently a teaching of the past. Differently means also going beyond! And this could be the meaning of an anniversary. But above all it is faithfulness to the tradition which makes us alive.

Translated by Liam & Patricia Kelly

Contributors

CHRISTOPH THEOBALD, SJ – Born in Cologne, Germany, in 1946, Christoph Theobold joined the Society of Jesus in 1978 and was ordained priest in 1982. He is professor of fundamental and dogmatic theology in the Jesuit faculties in Paris – Centre Sèvres, editor in chief of *Recherches de Science Religieuse*, member of the academic committee of the Istituto per le Scienze Religiose in Bologna, director of the collection Unam sanctam, Nouvelle série and of the French authorised critical edition of the works of Karl Rahner. He also advises various pastoral services of the Catholic Church in France.

Address: Facultés jésuites de Paris – Centre Sèvres, 35bis Rue de Sèvres, F-75006 Paris, France

Email: theobald.c@wanadoo.fr

MASSIMO FAGGIOLI – A member of Bologna's John XXIII Foundation between 1996 and 2008, Faggioli is currently ordinary professor in the Department of Theology and Religious Studies at Villanova University (Philadelphia, USA). His books include: *The Rising Laity. Ecclesial Movements since Vatican II* (Paulist Press, 2016); *La onda larga del Vaticano II. Por un nuevo posconcilio* (Universidad Alberto Hurtado: Santiago de Chile, 2017); *Cattolicesimo, nazionalismo, cosmopolitismo. Chiesa, società e politica dal Vaticano II a papa Francesco* (Rome: Armando Editore, 2018).

Address: Villanova University, Dept. of Theology and Religious Studies SAC 203, 800 Lancaster Avenue, Villanova, PA 19085, USA

Email: massimo.faggioli@villanova.edu

JAYEEL CORNELIO is the Director of the Development Studies Program at the Ateneo de Manila University, Philippines. He is currently a visiting professor at the Divinity School of Chung Chi College at the Chinese University of Hong Kong. His first book is *Being Catholic in*

the Contemporary Philippines: Young People Reinterpreting Religion (Routledge, 2016). With Jose Mario Francisco, SJ, he is currently writing a monograph on popular Christianity for Paulist Press. A co-editor of the journal *Social Sciences and Missions*, Cornelio was named one of the 2017 Outstanding Young Scientists of the Philippines.

Address: Director, Development Studies Program, Ateneo de Manila University, Loyola Heights, Quezon City, Philippines 1108
Email: jcornelio@ateneo.edu

VIRGINIA R. AZCUY is titular professor in the theology faculty of the Catholic University of Argentina and a researcher at the Centro Teológico Manuel Larraín at the Catholic university of Chile. She is co-author, with Nancy E. Bedford and Mercedes García Bachmann, of *Teología feminista a tres voces* (Santiago de Chile, 2016). With C. M. Galli and J. C. Caamaño she edited *La eclesiología del Concilio Vaticano II. Memoria, Reforma y Profecía* (Buenos Aires, 2015) and, with D. García and C. Schickendantz, *Lugares e interpelaciones de Dios. Discernir los signos de los tiempos* (Santiago de Chile, 2017).

Address: Facultad de Teología de la UCA, Concordia 4422, 1419 Buenos Aires, Argentina
Address 2: Facultad de Teología de la UC, Avda. Vicuña Mackenna 4860, Santiago, Chile
Email: aqazvi@gmail.com

STAN CHU ILO is a research Professor of Catholic Studies, African Studies and the World Church at the Center for World Catholicism and Intercultural Theology, DePaul University, Chicago, USA, where he coordinates the African Catholicism Project. He is the President of the Canadian Samaritans for Africa and the 2017 Recipient of the Afro-Excellence Award for Global Impact. His most recent book is *A Poor and Merciful Church: The Illuminative Ecclesiology of Pope Francis* and the entry in the *Oxford Handbook on Ecclesiology on African Roman Catholic Ecclesiology*.

Address: 3020 N. 76th Court, Elmwood Park, Illinois 60707, USA
Email: silo@depaul.edu

MIKE VAN TREEK is an independent biblical researcher, born in Chile in 1974. Doctorate in Theology by the Catholic University of Louvain at Louvain-la-Neuve (2008). Magister in Biblical Theology by the Gregorian University in Rome (2003). Assistant Professor, Faculty of Theology in the Pontifical Catholic University of Santiago, Chile (2003-2017). Author of *Expresión literaria del placer en la Biblia hebrea* (Verbo Divino, Madrid, 2010), and many essays, papers and columns. Orcid and RG profiles:

Web Address: http://orcid.org/0000-0003-4646-1956
Web Address 2:https://www.researchgate.net/profile/Mike_Van_Treek2/info
Address: Unión Obrera 530, Rancagua, Chile
Email: mvantreek@gmail.com

SERENA NOCETI – Full lecturer in systematic theology at the Istituto Superiore di Scienze Religiose in Florence; also teaches at the Facoltà teologica dell'Italia centrale. She is also a founding member of the Coordination of Italian Women Theologians and vice-president of the Italian Theological Association. Among her publications, which focus particularly on ecclesiology, the theology of gender and catechesis, are: S. DIENIC – S. NOCETI, *Trattato sulla chiesa*, Brescia 2002, 20153; M. PERRONI – A. MELLONI – S. NOCETI (ed.), *'Tantum aurora est'. Donne e Vaticano II*, Munich 2012; S. NOCETI (ed.), *Diacone. Quale ministero per quale chiesa?* Brescia 2017. She is also, with Roberto Repole, editor of the *Commentario ai documenti del Vaticano II*.

Address: Istituto Superiore di Scienze Religiose, Piazza Torquato Tasso, 1/A, 50124 Firenze FI, Italy
Email: serena.enne@gmail.com

DANIELLA ZSUPAN-JEROME Ph.D. is professor of pastoral theology at Notre Dame Seminary in New Orleans. She is the author of *Connected Toward Communion: The Church and Social Communication in the Digital Age* (Liturgical Press, 2014) and *Evangelization and Catechesis: Echoing the Good News Through the Documents of the Church* (Twenty-Third Publications, 2017) as well as of several articles and essays on the relationship between faith and digital culture, along with a number of pastoral and devotional resources. She is also co-editor of *Authority and*

Leadership: Values, Religion Media (Blanquerna Observatory, Barcelona, 2017).
Address: Notre Dame Seminary, 2901 S. Carrollton Ave, New Orleans, LA 70118, USA
Email: dzjerome@nds.edu

THIERRY-MARIE COURAU is a Professor at the Faculty of Theology and Religious Sciences – Theologicum, at the Catholic Institute of Paris, of which he was the Dean (2011-2017). He is a Dominican, and a Priest with a degree in Engineering and Business Management. He was elected President of the *International Journal of Theology – Concilium* – in June 2018. He is a delegate to the Buddhist authorities representing the Conference of Bishops of France, and his teachings, his research and his publications are on Buddhism and the theology of dialogue. *Paul VI and François. Salvation is dia-logue*, Paris, Cerf, 2018; *The exercises which lead to Buddhist Awakening*, Paris, Cerf, 2017, *The Fountains of Awakening*, Paris, Cerf, 2016.
Address: 222 rue du Faubourg Saint-Honoré, 75008 – Paris, France
Email: Tm.courau@icp.fr

GERARD MANNION holds the Amaturo Endowed Chair in Catholic Studies at Georgetown University. Founding chair of the Ecclesiological Investigations International Research Network, he has authored, co-authored and edited some nineteen books and numerous articles and chapters in the fields of ethics, ecclesiology, ecumenical and interreligious dialogue. He is presently the President of the International Network of Societies for Catholic Theology (INSeCT). Relative to this specific article, he has been a member of the AAR for sixteen years and was the joint founding chair of the Ecclesiological Investigations Program Unit of the AAR. He also helped establish the AAR's Vatican II Studies Program Unit.
Address: Department of Theology, Georgetown University, Room New North 120, Box 571135, 37th and O Streets, Washington DC 20057-1135, USA
Email: ges.mannion@gmail.com

GIANLUCA MONTALDI, born in 1966, obtained a doctorate in theology from the Pontifical Gregorian University with a thesis on the concept of faith at the Second Vatican Council. He has done both pastoral and educational work. He has published *In fide ipsa essentia revelationis completur*, Rome, 2015 and, with F. Bosin, has edited *Ridire il Credo oggi. Percorsi, sfide, proposte*, forthcoming. In 2017 he was elected secretary of the Italian Association for Theological Investigation.
   Address: Via F.lli Kennedy 12/a, 25030 Cizzago (BS), Italy
   Email: gianluca.montaldi@gmail.com

PIER LUIGI CABRI, a priest of the Congregation of the Sacred Heart of Jesus, is a graduate in philosophy and doctor of theology. He is lecturer in fundamental theology in the Facoltà teologica dell'Emilia Romagna and permanent lecturer at ISSR of Emilia in Modena. His publications include *Sulla difficile arte di amare. Con Lévinas e oltre Lévinas*, Bologna, 2011. He is currently director of *Edizioni Dehoniane* in Bologna.
   Address: via Scipione Dal Ferro 4, 40138 Bologna, Italy
   Email: pierluigi.cabri@dehoniane.it

ANTONIO AUTIERO is Professor emeritus, University of Münster (Germany), where he taught Moral Theology from 1991 to 2013. He received his doctoral degree in moral theology from the Accademia Alfonsiana (Rome) and was a fellow of the Foundation Alexander von Humboldt at the University of Bonn. Between 1997 and 2011, he directed the Center for Religious Studies of Trento (Italy). He has authored or edited numerous books and articles on fundamental moral theology, theories of the moral subject, and in the field of applied ethics. Autiero is a member of German Academy of Ethics in Medicine, of the StemCell Research governmental commission in Berlin, and of the Planning Committee of Catholic Theological Ethics in the World Church.
   Address: Paulstr. 18, D – 10557 Berlin, Germany
   Email: autiero@uni-muenster.de

CONCILIUM
International Journal of Theology

FOUNDERS
Anton van den Boogaard; Paul Brand; Yves Congar, OP; Hans Küng;
Johann Baptist Metz; Karl Rahner, SJ; Edward Schillebeeckx

BOARD OF DIRECTORS
President: Felix Wilfred
Vice Presidents: Erik Borgman; Diego Irarrázaval; Susan Ross

BOARD OF EDITORS
Mile Babić (Bosnia, Herzegovina Sarajevo)
Maria Clara (Bingemer, Brazil Rio de Janeiro)
Erik Borgman (The Netherlands, Tilburg)
Lisa Sowle (Cahill, USA Boston)
Thierry-Marie (Courau, France Paris)
Enrico Galavotti (Italy, Chieti Scalo)
Linda Hogan (Ireland, Dublin)
Huang, Po-Ho (Taiwan, Tainan)
Diego Irarrazaval (Chile, Santiago)
Leonard Santedi Kinkupu (Congo, Kinshasa)
Stefanie Knauss (Austria / USA Villanova)
Solange Lefebvre (Canada, Montreal)
Carlos Mendoza-Álvarez (Mexico, Mexico City)
Sarojini Nadar (South Africa, Durban)
Daniel Franklin Pilario (The Philippines, Quezon City)
Susan A. Ross (USA, Chicago)
Andres Torres Queiruga (Spain, Santiago de Compostela)
João J. Vila-Chã (Portugal / Italy Rome)
Marie-Theres Wacker (Germany, Münster)
Felix Wilfred (India, Chennai)

PUBLISHERS
SCM Press (London, UK)
Matthias-Grünewald Verlag (Ostfildern, Germany)
Editrice Queriniana (Brescia, Italy)
Editorial Verbo Divino (Estella, Spain)
EditoraVozes (Petropolis, Brazil)
Ex Libris and Synopsis (Rijeka, Croatia)

Concilium Secretariat:
Asian Centre for Cross-Cultural Studies,
40/6A, Panayur Kuppam Road, Sholinganallur Post, Panayur, Madras 600119, India.
Phone: +91- 44 24530682 Fax: +91- 44 24530443
E-mail: Concilium.madras@gmail.com
Managing Secretary: Arokia Mary Anthonidas

Concilium Subscription Information

December	**2018/5:**	*Ecology and Theology of Nature*
February	**2019/1:**	*Cities: Beyond the North-South Paradigm*
April	**2019/2:**	*Populism & Religion*
July	**2019/3:**	*TBA*
October	**2019/4:**	*TBA*

New subscribers: to receive the next five issues of Concilium please copy this form, complete it in block capitals and send it with your payment to the address below. Alternatively subscribe online at www.conciliumjournal.co.uk

Please enter my annual subscription for Concilium starting with issue 2017/2.

Individuals
_____ £50 UK
_____ £72 overseas and Eire
_____ $95 North America/Rest of World
_____ €85 Europe

Postage included – airmail for overseas subscribers

Payment Details:
Payment must accompany all orders and can be made by cheque or credit card
I enclose a cheque for £/$/€ _____ Payable to Hymns Ancient and Modern Ltd
Please charge my Visa/MasterCard (Delete as appropriate) for £/$/€ _____

Credit card number _____

Expiry date _____Card security number_____

Signature of cardholder_____

Name on card _____

Telephone _____E-mail _____

Send your order to *Concilium,* **Hymns Ancient and Modern Ltd**
13a Hellesdon Park Road, Norwich NR6 5DR, UK
E-mail: concilium@hymnsam.co.uk
or order online at www.conciliumjournal.co.uk

Customer service information
All orders must be prepaid. Your subscription will begin with the next issue of Concilium. If you have any queries or require Information about other payment methods, please contact our Customer Services department.